LOVE OF LIFE

LOVE OF LIFE
Autobiographical Sketches

William H. Beierwaltes, M.D.

VANTAGE PRESS
New York

To my parents, wife, and children

Contents

Appendixes   217

Introduction

How does a poor boy raised in a modest home in Saginaw, Michigan, eventually appear in Marquis's *Who's Who in the World* and *The Best Doctors in America* (Naifen and Smith) as well as receive the highest Scientific Achievement Award presented by the American Medical Association to one doctor in the United States in 1994?

Simultaneously he serves as skipper, first mate, or sailing master in seventeen Chicago-to-Mackinaw and Port Huron-to-Mackinaw races. He also serves as first mate in the 1960 Newport-to-Bermuda race (635 miles), experiencing the strongest wind ever recorded in the history of that race.

Simultaneously his life is sparked by: (1) His first date with Florence Schust, who appears and disappears in his life as she becomes one of the "17 most outstanding women in the United States" (*Harper's Bazaar*, 1967). (2) Larry Hagman (Mary Martin's son) living in his basement apartment for two weeks (prior to becoming famous as J. R. Ewing on *Dallas*). (3) Becoming a close friend of Robert McNamara for thirteen years as well as a daily associate of Dr. Jonas Salk (prior to his creating the Salk polio vaccine). (4) The adversities of *no pay*, Pearl Harbor, and World War II, and his being confined to bed for one year with tuberculosis during his medical internship, challenging a successful marriage and parenting of three children. (5) Pioneering the new medical specialty of nuclear medicine and publishing the first textbook in that specialty. (There are currently about 100,000 professionals attending nuclear medicine meetings all over the world.)

I have told these stories to friends. They have given me strong encouragement to write these "stories" for others to enjoy. I hope that these stories will show how exciting, funny, and rewarding life can be.

LOVE OF LIFE

The Beginnings

The Beginning

First Memories

Mother

My mother picked me up, carried me to the front porch, and yelled happily at the newspaper boy on the street. This is my earliest memory of my mother. September 17, 1918, was a sunny day. I was one year and ten months old. The front porch was at 910 Sheridan Avenue, Saginaw, Michigan. The paperboy had excited her by yelling, "Wuxtree! Wuxtree! Read all about the Armistice!" My mother was thirty-four years old. Her skin was flushed because of excitement. The cause of her excitement must have been that her husband would not have to go to war. World War I had already drained off most of her male relatives and friends, and my father was eligible to be drafted.

My global image memory of my mother was that she was always exciting, creative, and willing to try new things on the spur of the moment, usually with emotion. She gave freely of her intimacy. In retrospect, I can see that she passed these characteristics on to me and through me to our three children.

Father

I have no first image of my father. In retrospect, my global image of my father was and is that, although fun loving, he spent progressively more time, as he aged, sitting around thinking. When he did speak, it was obvious that he had thought thoroughly about the various aspects of the problem and how best to present his questions or views to instruct. Even when Mother had inadvertently scared us or hurt us or needed reorientation of her tact in an emergency, Dad would speak quietly and objectively on why we should all quiet down and easily resolve our latest problem.

3

Dad was also very ritualistic. Indeed, he was obsessive/compulsive in the routine of his days, at least later in life. He would come to the breakfast table every morning with his shoelaces and his tie not tied. If there was no toast waiting for him in the toaster, he would put it in himself and then burn it. When he turned the toaster upside down to get out the toast, the table would be covered with old black crumbs from inside the toaster. The implication was that Mother should have had the toast ready for him, perfectly done as he sat down. I also remember his telling Mother, much to my amazement, that when he said he wanted dinner at 6:00 P.M. he didn't mean 6:01 P.M.!

As soon as breakfast was over, he would finish dressing and walk about one mile to work at Mautner and Krause Clothing Store. As recently as two months ago when I attended my sixtieth class reunion, almost everyone I talked to from Saginaw, Michigan, mentioned that they had seen him when he was on his route to the Mautner and Krause Clothing Store and talked to him and admired the way he walked and everything about him. He would also walk home for lunch at twelve o'clock every day and walk back after one hour. Only when he got to be about seventy years of age and was thinking of retiring did he tell me that he was getting tired after lunch. I encouraged him to lie down immediately after lunch and have a little snooze.

Grandfather

Our father *never* struck us or said harsh words in disciplining us. Allegedly, this was because he had had a *tough* father who hit his kids when he got mad at them. My father's brothers told me later that, when their father struck them, their bodies flew across the room until they hit the opposite wall. All of them grew up with the strong conviction that it should be possible to raise a child without hitting him or her. They all succeeded in this desire. It is of interest, however, that, of his seven children, the majority had no children or just one child.

It is understandable that my father's father, Johann Sebastian Beierwaltes, was tough. He was born in a little German town named Steinwiesen, a two-hour drive north of Munich. He

4

ran away from a strict upbringing when he was twelve years of age to board a ship in London bound for New York. He was a stowaway in the engine room. He joined relatives in Chicago and got a job oiling locomotives. One day he threw his lunch pail into the Chicago River and "rode the rails" to a ranch in Texas (1865). He then served as a cowpuncher until General Custer recruited cowboys from the Texas ranchers for military duty in the Mexican wars. He left General Custer six months before the Little Big Horn massacre to return to his job as a cowpuncher on the original ranch.

Shipping cattle from the ranch area to the Chicago stockyards was often followed by a lower-than-expected cattle count upon arrival at the Chicago stockyards. The ranch owner for whom my grandfather worked asked him to accompany the herd of cattle he put on the train to Chicago twice a year. The purpose of this trip was for my grandfather to make certain that there was an accurate cattle count when the herd arrived in Chicago.

After a year or two, my grandfather found that the pay of the slaughterers in the Chicago stockyards was considerably higher than his. He then worked as a slaughterer in the Chicago stockyards. Soon, this new job led to his taking wholesale meat to Swift's packing house in Saginaw, Michigan, where he found he had some relatives.

We have a letter in his handwriting to some of our relatives in Germany stating that he was sound financially; he had a permanent pension from the United States government because he had fought with General Custer in the United States Army. He also was a section chief at Swift packing plant and actually wrote the letter on their stationery. Later, he founded a meat market a few blocks away in Saginaw, Michigan. This meat market became so successful that he also started a ham-smoking shed and purchased several houses around this establishment for him and his wife and his children. I am told that Mother and Father's first home was his gift to them, valued at about $2,000 at that time.

My grandfather then became president of the Michigan Meat Market Association. I am told by my father's brothers that he took trains with his wife to national meetings on the West Coast representing the butchers' union.

5

My father and his brothers were required to deliver meat before going to school and work for their father in their spare time. Dad then got a job as a clerk in a men's clothing store in downtown Saginaw (Mautner and Krause Clothing Corporation), on the corner of Genessee and Baum.

Of course, the main impression that my brother and I had of our grandfather was that, as a cowboy ranch hand in Texas in 1865, he had to be a classical cowboy with six-shooters on each hip ready to draw as necessary to defend himself.

Mother's Frustrations and Strengths

Mother would sometimes become frustrated with me (or life?) and "spank" me with a three-foot rubber garden hose. This hurt so much that I would cry. This all ended when I reached about twelve years of age. One day I took the hose out of her hands and threw it away (where she would not find it) as I "ran away from home." I also "announced" to her that I was too old for her to spank me anymore.

Friends of my mother (and she had lots of good friends) told me that, after having my older brother Jack, she wanted a girl so badly that she cried when she got a second (and last) child who was also a boy (me) on November 23, Thanksgiving Day, 1916.

The impression that Mother conveyed to us was that she was raised by her older sister, Em, because her mother had died when she was very young and her father was irresponsible and ran off to the Upper Peninsula to work in the copper mines.

When I got to be about fifty and was suddenly interested in discovering and pinning down our "roots," I found out, much to my surprise, that Mother had underevaluated the Aris family (her paternal family of origin).

Grandfather Aris

At a New Year's Eve party at the University of Michigan, in a close friend's house, I introduced myself to a new guest and found that his name was Aris! He was a professor of business administration at the University of Michigan Business School. I told him that if his name was Aris he must be a relative of mine. At first, he was upset to hear this wild statement from someone who had just finished a drink. I quickly established, however, that indeed he was a cousin of mine. I told him that Mary-Martha, my wife, and I were going to fly to London shortly and we wondered if he could give us any background on the Aris family. He said that he was not interested in the family genealogy but his brother (who was a professor of economics at Albion College in Michigan) was intensely interested in genealogy and had a handwritten description of the Aris family. I called and wrote this very nice man, and he provided me with a written description of the Aris family. The Arises were farmers in England and about seven of them came to what is now South-field, Michigan, to establish seven farms there. Allegedly, their farms were what now constitute downtown Southfield, Michigan. Oh, how I wish that I had the property that they sold to sell today!

This professor was not particularly interested in my Grandfather Aris, and so it was impressive to have him clearly outline why Grandfather Aris was perhaps the most successful of all these farm families. He first developed a grocery store to sell his produce. This operation became so successful that he then established a meat market and a ham-smoking place. He was so successful financially that he decided to go to the Upper Peninsula, where men were quickly becoming millionaires acquiring and running copper mines. He did not succeed in becoming a millionaire there, and my grandmother and grandfather eventually bought a small house, on Bagley Street, a mile or so from our house at 910 Sheridan Avenue. They lived there until she died and then he. He died at about age eighty-six. He walked the mile to our house once or twice a week to have dinner with us. My last memories of him are of him playing checkers with me: I would have to awaken him after I made my move. He would then sit up, look at the board, and jump about five of my kings and take them away. He was a very pleasant person to be with in his eighties.

Great-Grandfather Aris

Later, when I was about sixty and invited to be a visiting professor at Oxford University in England, my host asked me what I wanted to do in my spare time. I told him that I did not know what my mother's side of the family did. We went to the library and my host found that my mother's grandfather was a graduate of Oxford University in about 1825 with a degree in music and had become the head of music for the Church of England! It is regrettable that my mother never learned how successful her mother's and father's sides of the family had been.

Mother and Mrs. Mautner

Before marrying my father, Mother had been a "typewriter" at Wick Brothers Hardware Corporation in Saginaw. Later, during her marriage, she became very active in several women's organizations. It was at one of these meetings that she met Mrs. Mautner (of Mautner and Krause Clothing Corporation). Mrs. Mautner was a delightful person who was very social. She and Mother hit it off together immediately. Mrs. Mautner made several inquiries about my father's salary and how well the salary suited their needs. Mrs. Mautner was astounded that her husband and his partner paid Dad so little. Within two months, Dad had received a very significant pay raise. Mrs. Mautner and Mother continued their happy association. We still have the huge beautiful oak rocking chair that the Mautners gave Mother and Dad for a wedding present in 1909. We still have it in 1994, and we have rocked our children and grandchildren in it many times as we read them many books. When Mr. Mautner died, he left his controlling interest in the Mautner and Krause Clothing Corporation to Dad. This was a great and happy surprise to Dad but not a surprise to Mother.

"Programming" of Bill

Every day that Dad went to work when I was a little child,

he would outline the tasks around the house he expected me to complete before his return home. When he came home, he praised me for what I had accomplished and let me know how important that was to me, him, and the family as a unit. These activities must have started my work habits that became a major part of making my career.

My Brother Jack

My father also started my older brother, Jack, on a magazine route and selling *Shoppers News*. Jack was always an outstanding salesman and rapidly built up a good roster of steady customers for his magazines. When Jack became old enough to work in Mautner and Krause Clothing Store in his spare time, before going to the University of Michigan and while attending the university, I inherited all the magazine and *Shoppers News* routes. I will never forget Schirmer's Drug Store, only a few blocks from our house. When I went in to sell Mr. Schirmer a *Liberty* magazine, he was very nice to me and bought the magazine, but as I left, he threw it on his pile of *Liberty* magazines that he had for sale.

Jack soon found a more profitable job doing door-to-door sales on commission for a lumber company in Saginaw. He began to realize his capabilities as a salesman and astounded me first when he purchased a Model-A Ford with a rumble seat secondhand for $250. Rumble-seat kissing of dates was great fun for all of us at that age at that time.

The Importance of a College Education

Jack and I enjoyed working in the store with the "older" clerks and suggested to Dad that we work there as a career. Dad made it clear that each generation had to do better than the last. Since Dad and Mother had not gone to college, Dad stressed that Jack and I were to have that great privilege. He gave me numerous little "sermons" on how grateful we all were that, by each of us working hard to make it possible, Jack and I

9

were to enjoy the greatest privilege, namely the privilege of learning at the University of Michigan. Dad also could never understand why anyone in college should have to stay up the night before an examination to study. It would be so much fun to learn daily that we would have learned our lessons well day by day. His little "sermons" did affect all my habits.

The First Bicycle

I had one of the first bicycles on the campus at the University of Michigan (secondhand, of course) to enable to me get to my board job and to classes and then to the law library or to the Rackham post-graduate building or the general library to study without interruption. I studied every night and all day Saturday and Sunday (except for board job and dates) so that I would go to bed at the usual time of 11:30 P.M., including the night before an examination. I also have nothing but pleasant memories of learning daily in a highly organized fashion.

Mr. Mautner and Mr. Krause

In early childhood, I was often invited by Mr. Mautner and Mr. Krause to run downtown after school to "the store" to get money from either of these partners to go to the latest cowboy movie two doors away. Although the black-and-white movies were silent, the besplendored organist sat at a huge bespangled organ that would elevate at the push of a button and put the organist into a vari-colored spotlight during the appropriate intermission. The organ music also was played during all the key times of the movies. Thus, the organ music kept in time and added appropriate emotional tone, etc., to the various scenes.

Mr. Krause and Mr. Mautner also gave me money to buy a hot dog and a soft drink for the movie. After the movie I would occasionally be given a "silver dollar" with obvious love. I would then walk home with my father. He walked daily to work, home for lunch, back to work, and then home to family.

Seventh Grade—Charlie Christie

Was Charlie Christie the best junior high school teacher in the world?

In case you believe you have experienced the best, let me first tell you about Charlie. If you believe your teacher was better, certainly I, and probably the majority of other people, would like to hear all about your nomination for the competition.

In 1928, when I was in the sixth grade at Emerson Elementary School (grades 1–6) in Saginaw, Michigan, I had already heard wonderful things about Charlie Christie. He was the "woodwork" junior high school teacher (grades 7–9). My older brother, Jack, and his best friend, Fred Klein, were in the eighth grade and were becoming inspired and skilled boat builders under Charlie's spell.

The Model Boat Club

Charlie had a "boat club" that anyone could join if he would come after school to work on the boat he was building. Charlie had designed and built a boat every two years since he was seventeen years of age. In retrospect, I would guess he was sixty years old when I met him in 1929. He was a perfectionist but had a subtle but well-developed sense of humor. He obviously was knowledgeable, not only in woodworking, but also in just about everything there was to know about boats. He was bright and right. He subscribed to *Yachting* and *Rudder* magazines and constantly wrote "how to" articles that were published in *Motor Boating*. These articles were on such topics as how to make a watertight companionway, how to make a watertight mast step, etc. Allegedly, he wrote these to win a prize of special

11

boat equipment or cash that enabled him to build new boats on a very limited teacher's income.

The "Boats" the Students Made and How

My older brother, Jack, started out building a sailing model of a twenty-one-foot sloop sailboat with a little cabin on it. This was called *Gozo*. Next was a gaff-rigged fisherman schooner and finally the *Nina*, a staysail schooner. If there were no line drawings or tables of offset, Christie called the architect as soon as he read the article in *Yachting* and asked for the necessary line drawings, etc., so that his students could make models of this boat. He told the architect who designed the *Nina* that it was his belief that this would become one of the most famous ocean racers in history. It was understandable to me that the architect would send Christie what he needed to teach kids how to build beautiful sailing models of these boats.

When I was in my fifties, I read an article in *Yachting* complete with the pictures documenting that the *Nina* had become an all-time, long-time winner under its one owner—DeCoursey Sales. She is also discussed in my chapter on the 1960 Newport-to-Bermuda race.

Christie would show each student how to glue together four to eight one-inch-thick, soft, white pine planks cut roughly to the approximate length and width of the boat to be. He would then show us individually how to draw lines, let us say one inch apart from end to end and from side to side on this glued-together block of wood to describe the tapering of the boat from side to side. He would then teach us how to use a hand-held draw plane and other tools to take off the extra wood from the outer shell of the boat with the boat held upside down so that another one-inch board five or six inches long on edge could be glued and screwed to what would eventually become the deck so that the boat could be held upside down in a vise clamped onto that board.

When the bottom and sides of the boat had been rounded to Christie's satisfaction, we were then taught to make a cradle for the boat to sit in upright in a vise while we chiseled all the wood out of the boat until the hull was translucent. The wooden part of the boat that formed the beginning of the keel on the bottom of the boat then received from us molten lead that had been poured into a mold to make a lead keel that could be glued and screwed or bolted through the keelson to the bottom of the boat. This furnished the external ballast and proper weight fore and aft for perfect sailing characteristics of the boat under sail.

The boat was then kept upright in the wooden cradle while we marked up on a sheet of plywood what looked like a planked deck. We then attached the deck to the edges of the hull with glue.

When I built my model Cape Cod catboat, my greatest thrill was to make bunks and centerboard box and table in front of the companionway steps coming down from the deck behind this table. Of course, I had to make appropriate pots and pans. We then made the cabins out of suitable one-eighth-inch plywood and made portholes through the sides of the cabin for light inside the boat.

The mast was then tapered out of wood dowels and fitted through the deck into the inner hull. "Shrouds" were used to hold the mast up in the midline. These shrouds were made to attach to the sides of the boat and to the top of the mast and also to the bow of the boat and the stern.

We then flattened lead BBs (for a BB gun) and drilled holes in them to perfectly simulate pulleys for the halyards with which to pull up the sails. Similar "blocks" were made for the "sheet ropes" to trim in the sails from side to side. Cleats to fasten these "lines" were made out of suitable "tailor-made" tin cans. Rudder posts, rudder, tiller, and "wheels" similarly were made by the student to perfectly simulate essentials for steering large boats.

After varnishing the decks and cabin and painting the hull of the boat with water lines, etc., we then took them into the water and suitably adjusted the sails, etc. to make certain that these sailboats sailed perfectly. They had always been designed so that they felt light but "stiff" to stand up suitably in the wind without the boat leaning over too far. Of course, the boats had to be fast and seaworthy.

When we had our sixtieth high school class reunion in Saginaw on September 19, 1994, I asked numerous old friends at social gatherings if any of them had been in Christie's model boat class and had made boats. Much to my surprise, everyone that I talked to had made at least one boat and all still had them. Bob Beckley had made a J-boat model. (The 100- to 125-foot sailboats, such as the *Endeavor* and *Ranger*, etc., that were popular for the International America's Cup against England were of this type.)

But that was not all: many of these junior high school students went on to build bigger boats, with designs and encouragement by Christie.

My brother made an 8-by-3½-foot sailing pram with oars and a centerboard box. Jack and I, with the encouragement of our father, rowed that boat in one day from Saginaw, Michigan, out the Saginaw River for twenty miles to Saginaw Bay and then across seven miles of the lower end of Saginaw Bay to our cottage at Killarney Beach. Later, my brother graciously gave that pram to me for my first "get in" sailboat.

My brother wanted to build a new hydroplane speedboat powered by an outboard engine. The price he had to pay to fulfill this dream was to earn the money working at my father's clothing store and to make the boat himself from Christie's plans in the barn of a friend (Walt Carmen) who lived nearby. It took him all winter to complete it. He put a Kaillie outboard engine on the transom, and the boat was fast. The propeller threw a plume of water up about eight feet behind the transom that extended out behind the boat for about twenty feet. Everyone on Killarney Beach wanted to ride in it.

Jack's friend, Fred Klein, made a Christie-designed fourteen-foot flat-bottom sloop with a cockpit and a small cuddy cabin, the *Flying Dutchman*. The sloop was gaff-rigged with a centerboard. Christie served as a most interested and proud consultant to Fred Klein.

When Fred graduated from junior high and moved over to Saginaw High School (about four blocks away), he then graduated to making a twenty-two-foot cutter sloop with a cabin and called the *Meteor*. I can still see him shaping out the "keelson" on the bottom of the boat with a potentially very dangerous axe-type chisel called an "adze." Properly trained by Christie, Fred

14

never hurt himself. I later remember Jack helping Fred sail this "big" cabin boat across Saginaw Bay from north to south in a strong "northeaster," getting him back from the Bay City Yacht Club long after dark. His story of this trip excited my imagination.

But that was not all. Christie built a thirty-two-foot power cruiser and took it out the Saginaw River into Saginaw Bay frequently on weekends. He often invited some of his most interested and interesting students to bring their parents for a Sunday afternoon outing. This outing included swimming, eating, and especially sailing his latest light and fast sailing dinghy that he had designed and built.

Christie Advocates Annapolis

But that was not all: Christie was consulted by students and parents on the best method for a student to train for the best career that related to boats. I never heard Christie say so, but "the word" passed around was that we should go to Annapolis. I have no idea how many of his students became captains in the Navy, but in a few years several friends of ours within a few blocks of our house launched into successful careers with little or no money but with great vigor and success.

Outcome of His Students—1994

Harry Jackson, my closest friend and classmate, worked his way through the University of Michigan School of Naval Architecture and Marine Engineering. He was then commissioned in the navy and participated in the development of antisubmarine vessels so desperately needed to sink the German submarine fleet. He then became a captain in the navy and headed the largest floating dry dock in the Pacific Ocean from 1943 to 1946. At age seventy-seven, he currently teaches at the Massachusetts Institute of Technology in Boston and does consulting work in deep-ocean technology on a worldwide basis. He lectured at Annapolis on several occasions. In December 1993, he

15

was a member of the Engineering Accreditation Board to approve or disapprove the engineering accreditation of the academy.

In 1980, Harry was awarded the highest medal from the American Society of Naval Engineers and in September 1993 he received the highest medal from the Society of Naval Architects and Marine Engineers.

Another classmate of ours, Erwin Rhode, also received the same medals. Erwin now lives in Boston, MA.

Fred Klein joined the navy and in 1942 entered the lighter-than-air program. He became the commander of the last active blimp squadron. He was the base commander of the Lakehurst Naval Air Station at the time of his retirement. One of his greatest enjoyments was his beautifully restored, antique Gar Wood speedboat. He was buried in Arlington National Cemetery on November 12, 1993.

Keats Montross was a close and very handsome friend of my brother Jack in junior high school with Christie. Keats graduated from Annapolis and became the youngest United States submarine captain in World War II. He married, had children, and was most effective in sinking Japanese ships until he was sunk by the Japanese with all hands aboard.

Why did I not go to Annapolis? My friends told me that you had to be a good mathematician to get through Annapolis. I did not think that I was good enough. In addition, in the tenth grade, I was excited by a woman biology teacher. I reasoned that the highest biology was man, and so I worked my way through seven years of the University of Michigan to get an M.D. degree and could not have made a better choice.

Christie's Contract to Build My Snipe

However, I never escaped Charlie Christie. We were taking both *Yachting* and *Rudder* magazines from junior high school on. When I was in the tenth grade, my brother Jack came to me one day and said with great excitement, "Bill, let me show you the design of the new open racing sailboat that you must have immediately. You must build it and race it." It was called the *Snipe*.

My father had greater confidence in Christie's experience and Christie's ability to build a boat than he had in me. Dad was "a legend in frugality." He was thus able to buy the *Flying Dutchman* from Fred Klein when it was several years old and when minnows were able to swim in and out of the cracks in the bottom. Nevertheless, although a thirteen-foot flat-bottom sloop, it had a beautifully rounded cockpit like a yacht and a cuddy cabin with doors on it. It was, of course, a very good sailor and the first real honest-to-goodness sailboat I had ever had. It was my first opportunity to become a good sailor.

Since Dad was a legend in frugality, he offered Fred Klein the opportunity to sell the *Flying Dutchman* by taking it out in "buying" new clothes from his clothing store. Since there was a 40 percent corporate markup on all clothes, this allowed him to acquire the *Flying Dutchman* for me at only sixty percent of the $25.

Similarly, he told Christie that he could only afford to pay $45 to have him build the *Snipe*, including materials. Christie, of course, recognized that this boat would be one of the most outstanding racing classes in the world and that it would be a wonderful learning experience for me to build it. He therefore used the $45 to buy the best redwood (good wood for immersion in water but splits much more easily than cedar or mahogany or teak).

Nevertheless, the following conditions had to be met: (1) Bill Beierwaltes would come to his home after school and on weekends until the boat was completed. Thus, under Christie's supervision, I first had to assist him in putting the hull together. (2) I would assist him in building and putting in the centerboard box, the deck, the rudder, and the tiller. (3) I would go down and get the steel plate for the centerboard and bring it to his house. (4) I would then make the mast, the boom, the sails, and the fittings. (5) I would then paint and rig the boat.

When we came to the metal fittings (cleats), pulleys, etc., my father said he could not pay for them. Christie then told me I would have to learn how to become a pattern maker. This

17

expertise makes wooden molds to be used in casting things in manganese bronze. He told me how difficult this would be, that it might take months and that pattern makers were considered highly trained and expensive specialists.

When I had finished the patterns, he asked me to see a specific foreman in a specific foundry in Saginaw and show him the patterns and tell him that I had made them over four months, that I had no money but knew that the fittings had to be cast in manganese bronze because Christie told me so. Now that I am older, I realize the emotion that the foreman felt when he realized that this tenth-grader had become an expert pattern maker under the tutelage of Charlie Christie. He cast them for pennies and I then perfected them over the next few months. Thus, I completed *Snipe* #2.

Gus Guthouse and Eric Tims

My next-door neighbors at the cottage, Gus Guthouse and family, were a tremendous asset. Gus had been a professional sailing yacht racer captain in Germany for years. He showed me how to splice steel cable to steel cable, make eyes, splice steel to rope, etc. He showed me how to tune the rigging and then took me out in Saginaw Bay for a series of exercises on the fundamentals leading to racing. The Tims family also lived in that cottage. Eric Tims (who later became one of two FBI agents who cracked the largest German spy ring in history and was on the cover of *Life* magazine) helped me sail the *Snipe* across thirty-two miles of Saginaw Bay to Point Lookout and then eighteen miles across Lake Huron to Tawas Bay. My friend, Bob Beckley, and I did it the first time in strong winds and won the Tawas Bay Class B Yachting Association trophy.

Eric Tims helped me take it back a second time in an attempt to defend the trophy.

The Barton Boat Club

Most of the next ten years were spent pursuing a career

working my way through seven years at the University of Michigan and interning and starting a residency at Cleveland Metropolitan Hospital. When I returned to Ann Arbor, the least expensive and best place to race was on Barton Pond at the Barton Boat Club. The boat to get was a second-hand Rhodes Bantam.

The *Thistle*

Although we had the usual very small academic salary, my wife and I finally saved up $800 and bought a seventeen-foot open centerboard racer called the *Thistle*. This was designed and built by Sandy Douglas. I invited two of my male friends to cruise the North Channel with me in that boat. The North Channel is situated at the top of Lake Huron in Canada, and many believe that it is the most beautiful cruising ground in the world. We did many innovative things in preparation for and on this cruise, and the article submitted to *Yachting* magazine was published as my first draft with pictures in the December 1955 issue, "Thistling North Channel."[1] The acceptance letter from the magazine included a certified check for $100!

The next day after publication, the commodore of the Bay View Yacht Club in Detroit (the sponsor of the Port Huron-Mackinaw race yearly) called me to tell me how much he enjoyed my article in *Yachting* magazine. He then wondered if I could bring slides and movies to lecture to the Bay View Yacht Club. They were particularly intrigued by the fact that we had cruised for two weeks in a seventeen-foot open racing sailboat with no outboard motor and had originated many new tricks in how to do this comfortably.

---

1. William H. Beierwaltes, "Thistling the North Channel," *Yachting* 98 (Dec. 1955): 58–98.

Subsequent Recreational Boating

Two days after the commodore of the Bay View Yacht Club had called me, an ex-medical-fraternity brother of mine, John Pierpont, called me from the Upper Peninsula of Michigan. He said that he had read my article in *Yachting* and wondered if I would be his first mate on a 42-foot Swedish ocean racer he had purchased in Detroit and had in the Apostle Islands in Lake Superior. He said it was his plan to race in both the Port Huron-Mackinaw and Chicago-Mackinaw races. My wife said, "Yes, go ahead and accept. I don't want a disconsolate husband staring out the windows at the sky while he's obviously missing the opportunity to be first mate on an ocean racer in the Mackinaw races."

This eventually led to my being the first mate on this boat in the Newport-to-Bermuda race (635 miles, 600 miles out in the Atlantic Ocean) in 1960. That race, the twenty-second, was the greatest excitement of my life because we sailed successfully through the strongest wind ever recorded in the history of that race. Several books were published on that race. Perhaps the best was *A Berth to Bermuda* by Bill Robinson, the editor of *Yachting* (see chapter titled, "The Ultimate Race").

Next, I was contacted by the vice president in charge of medical affairs at General Electric, who was trained in cardiology at the University of Michigan. I advised him to purchase a forty-one-foot Concordia yawl, which had won Bermuda races. He bought it, named it *Taloa* and attracted me off John Pierpont's *Siskiwit* by offering me the position of not only first mate but also sailing master.

For all these races, I furnished top-notch small boat racers from the Barton Boat Club members who were my friends. We later chartered our own forty-one-foot Owens cutter (*Candide*) from Chuck Coe of the Bay View Yacht Club and raced it in the Port Huron-Mackinaw race.

Later, we bought a Columbia 36 (*Windsong*) to compete against the Cal 36. We raced a few Mackinaw races in that with our kids. The group of us then collaborated to cruise the North Channel for thirteen consecutive years. Later, we actively participated in chartering in the Grenadines, British Virgin

Islands, the Bahamas, the Maine coast, the Caribbean, the Aegean Sea, and Tahiti. After my first retirement at age seventy from working at two hospitals in Detroit, we bought a thirty-four-foot auxiliary sloop (*Yet to Be*) that we sailed out of the Detroit Yacht Club on the Detroit River into Lake St. Clair. We also cruised Lake Erie. We then sold it on August 30, 1993.

Christie's Influence on His Students

I am obviously still reminded of Charlie Christie daily. Recently, when I was talking with Harry Jackson about getting a picture of Charlie Christie, I asked him how many model boats he had made under the influence of Christie. He said he had no idea, but he did know that he had a room full of them and was still continuing to make model boats. He also keeps a Friendship Sloop in front of his house in Connecticut and sails it on Long Island Sound.

I am not certain that I know the answer to why Charlie Christie had such a strong positive influence on such a large number of his students. Perhaps it was because he encouraged a large number of relatively poor boys to do something that they could afford that was highly charismatic. He also obviously taught us that perhaps all things are possible if they are done thoughtfully with the help of a great teacher. He also taught us that the closer to perfection of our product, the prouder we would be of our work and competitiveness of the product we had produced. For a large percent of his students, it encouraged them to go into a specific marine field and make substantial contributions to the general welfare of humanity. For those of us who did not go into a specific marine field, it gave us an opportunity at all levels of income to have wonderful recreation and to help us achieve contributions in such fields as medicine.

I have often wondered what would happen to the United States if every junior high school teacher had such a dramatic and important effect on so many children.

Eighth Grade

My First Date—Florence Schust

I constantly advise our grandchildren to never underestimate any child in their school and classes. It never occurred to me, when I had my first date in 1929 at age thirteen, that Florence Schust would become "one of the seventeen most outstanding women in the United States," according to a special supplement marking the centennial year of the oldest women's publication in the United States. *Harper's Bazaar* magazine spotlighted women leaders "outstanding in government, communications, art, theater, business, philanthropy, fashions, and home arts—symbolic of scores of outstanding women nationally."

Roller Skating Party

In the eighth grade, my closest friend, walking to and from school daily, was George Hillman. He was a handsome, charming, intelligent friend who also was feeling just a little restless with our career choice of several years to become cowboys. Perhaps it was the strong influence of Douglas Fairbanks Sr. movies introducing the excitement of the whip that Zorro had used to snatch cigarettes out of the mouth of villains and to escape desperate situations by snapping the end of his whip around a branch of a tree so that he could quickly climb out of an antagonistic crowd effortlessly.

Also, Charlie Christie's devotees had made it clear that scientific yachting and Annapolis and becoming a captain in the navy were perhaps the more mature ways to go.

One beautiful evening in June 1929, when I was thirteen

years old and in the eighth grade, George Hillman smilingly skated to our back door at 910 Sheridan Avenue on roller skates. I said, "George, what's up?"

He replied, "Bill, get on your roller skates. You and I are going to round up some other kids and go roller skating."

I said, "George, that is for children. We stopped that at the end of the sixth grade."

He said, "Yes, but tonight we're each going to have a date with a *girl* and skate together for a *date!*"

A wave of acute anxiety hit me, and I said, "George, I have never had a date, and I'm afraid of girls. Have you chosen a date for me? If so, who is she?"

George told me that she was our classmate in the eighth grade, Florence Schust. She lived about five blocks from my house, and I remembered that she was attractive and had bangs and page-boy styled black hair. Furthermore, George seemed to have everything well organized into a good group, so my anxiety began to subside.

We all had a good time skating out about two or three miles to the Saginaw Zoo. We sat around all talking to each other for about an hour or two and then skated back.

Subsequent Social Development—Early Stages

My always observant mother must have seen that it was time for me to develop my skills in associating with young ladies, such as learning to dance. Some of my friends had already been assigned by their parents to start dance lessons. My father, the legend in frugality, made it clear that there were other methods of achieving this goal that did not require paying for private dance lessons. Mother therefore made inquiries at junior high school and found that an afternoon dance was soon to occur.

I was too shy to get a date or even go alone, and so Mother took me to the dance. The rest was relatively painless because a very strong and attractive classmate of mine, Beatrice Charlton, immediately came up to me and pulled me out onto the gymnasium dance floor. When I explained to her that we couldn't do

23

this because I couldn't dance, she explained that there was nothing hard about dancing and she would personally teach me. Fortunately, there were other girls who were also very kind to me that afternoon, so that my mother never had to take me again.

Also, at that time, the Warren Avenue Presbyterian church did not have a social program for early teen kids, and "all of my friends" were going to a good program at the Congregational church where the social life was developing at breathtaking speed.

By the ninth grade, we had a very well-developed social clique, which met for dancing, etc., at someone's house on Friday and/or Saturday night every week all through junior and senior high (and in subsequent high school class reunions).

In retrospect, we all had a good time together and never felt lonely.

Furthermore, the city of Saginaw encouraged the big downtown city auditorium to bring in all the big bands and made it easy for all high school kids to bring dates by charging no more for a couple than for a single person.

It was understandable that a large number of kids from Saginaw High School (Eastern), Arthur Hill High School (west side), Bay City Handy Senior High School, and Bay City Junior College came to these dances. Indeed, the last time I attended a dance at the city auditorium before departing for the University of Michigan for seven years of working my way through undergraduate school and medical school, I decided to try to see how many people I could remember at the dance by at least their first names. The number was 350.

Ninth Grade

Lead in Class Play

In the ninth grade, I was thrown in with Florence Schust again. I had never seen her at any of the social events I have just outlined.

The male head of English and drama in junior high school taught us a little debating and lots of Shakespeare. He drafted me to be student traffic officer with a big bronze badge and to be the lead in the ninth-grade class play, "A Strenuous Life."

My mother fortunately placed in my photograph album a ten-by-seven-inch black-and-white photo of a scene in that play with fifteen people on stage. She also wrote identifying names, dates, my age, etc., on the back of that photo immediately.

Florence Schust was one of the people in the picture. She was not my leading lady, but she was the number two lady in the group. I notice that Bonnie Milne (relative of George Hillman and his next-door neighbor) was also in the play. She had been my secret love in grades 1 through 6 and bears a striking resemblance to Florence in all respects in the picture. I also remember that one rainy afternoon (while in the fifth grade) George "married" Bonnie and me while I sat on a bicycle in his garage.

Florence Goes to Kingswood

According to *Who's Who in America* in the 1990–91 edition, Florence was born in Saginaw on May 24, 1917, and therefore would have been thirteen years of age in that class play. Most of us in Saginaw remember that Florence's parents were killed in an automobile crash in Cuba the following year. It was a popular statement that she had an aunt who took over. Her article in *Oui* magazine of January 13–20, 1986, states that she was known to her friends as "Schu" and was brought up as a ward of a bank, which sent her to Kingswood, a girls' school in Bloomfield Hills, Michigan. At any rate, the Kingswood School had been designed by the famous architect Eliel Saarinen, as part of the Cranbrook Foundation.

Influence of Eliel Saarinen

Fascinated by the building, Florence attracted the attention of Eliel Saarinen whose son, Eero Saarinen, was studying architecture at Yale University. The family virtually adopted her, taking her along on their summer holidays in Finland.

Florence went on to study architecture at the Architectural Association in London, England in 1938–39, got a Bachelor of Arts in architecture at the Illinois Institute of Technology in Chicago in 1941, and studied at Columbia University in New York. In Chicago, Florence studied under Ludwig Mies Van der Rohe. Working in New York, she met and married Hans Knoll, the founder of Knoll Furniture Company and unequalled promoter of avant-garde design furniture.

Knoll International

Florence became design director of the firm and enlisted her long-time architectural friends, including Eero Saarinen and Mies Van der Rohe, to help create an entirely new concept in modern furniture production. The company turned out pieces that today are considered classics—the Saarinen chair and pedestal, the "Mies" Barcelona chair and sculptor Harry Bertoia's wire chair. Knoll became a mecca for young designers. Florence stressed that she had always been part of a team wherever she had been as well as doing things on her own.

She stated, "When Knoll was first a company, we credited designers with their names on the designs instead of just showing the name of the company. We gave people credit." She also

26

favored the creative approach to problem solving. Eero Saarinen's womb chair, which Florence had asked him to design, turned out to be impossible for any furniture manufacturer to produce.

So, Saarinen and Knoll tried a company that built fiberglass boats. "We found a boat builder in New Jersey who thought we were out of our minds. He had all these great big molds for the hulls of boats. He needed a lot of convincing that we were serious, but in the end we produced the chairs," Florence recalls.

Knoll's international division also came as a solution to a unique set of problems. "We were asked to furnish prefabricated houses for State Department personnel who were being sent to remote places overseas. The government wanted to pay for the supplies with wooden dollars, American money which was reserved in Europe and couldn't be taken out of the country. We started with a woodworking plant in Stuttgart, a metal foundry in Paris, and an accessories shop in Milan. That was the triangle I traveled a great deal."

Bassett and Miami

In 1955, Hans Knoll was killed in an automobile crash. Florence then became president of Knoll International. By this time they had established twenty-eight franchises. She began to tire of the big business role. Two years later she took a job designing the executive offices of the First National Bank in Miami. There she met and married its up-and-coming officer, Harry Hood Bassett, who in 1967 organized the SouthEast Banking Corporation, using as a foundation the First National Bank of Miami. She stated in her article in *Oui* that today the whole face of Miami is changing completely. Miami is emerging as a world class city with distinguished architects like I. M. Pei, Obata and Skidmore, Owings and Merrill. Noguchi redesigned the bay-front park and a new government center was built downtown designed by Philip M. Johnson.

Florence contributed to that change with the building of the SouthEast Financial Center. The building was designed by

Skidmore, Owings and Merrill, but it is obvious to anyone who knows her that this is Florence Bassett's baby. She and her husband went with the architect to Italy in 1983 to inspect a granite and glass mock-up of the building's facade. Working with the architect, she participated in all phases of the design.

Donning a hard hat, helping to draft plans during the construction, and later working on scale models of each room, she was involved in all details of construction.

When I was a visiting professor of internal medicine and nuclear medicine at the University of Miami in 1982, my hosts knew that I loved sailing and racing sailboats and so they took Mary-Martha and me for a sail on a Cal 36 that had been on the cover of *Yachting* magazine because it had won the southern ocean racing circuit. I told my friends this story while sailing parallel to the Miami coast and asked them if they'd ever heard of Florence Schust Knoll Bassett.

They all said everyone knew about Florence and knew that she had continued to participate, particularly in the interior design of a large number of the best buildings in Miami. They said, "You see that city on shore? Florence and her husband own almost the southern two-thirds of that city and live on Sunset Isle #1."

The article in *Oui* in 1986, when Florence was sixty-eight, said that she has always known precisely what she likes. Her favorite view of Miami was from the fifty-fifth story penthouse of the sleek granite and glass SouthEast Financial Center, which she helped design. It is the tallest building in Florida. Twenty stories below are the executive suites where her husband, Harry Hood Bassett, retired chairman of the SouthEast Banking Corporation, had his office. The article said that Florence Bassett had waited a long time for this view. In 1958, when she married and moved to Miami, the city was little more than a sun-drenched resort town. Bassett had left the Manhattan skyline and a career spent working in the forefront of modern design.

This article stated that she retains a style of uncluttered elegance in her own life. It said she likes her jewels big, bold and simply set, like the perfectly cut, dime-sized emerald and sapphire solitaires she wears on each hand. It said her car was a snappy red Mazda RX-7. Her condominium on an island over-looking Key Biscayne, bought when the Bassetts sold their estate, was furnished with the thirty-year-old originals she produced at Knoll.

"When the Bassetts are not in Miami, they usually go to the Vermont farmhouse she designed or to his ranch in Okeechobee, a farming town in central Florida. Their favorite night spot is the Biscayne Bay Yacht Club where the Bassetts usually order charcoal-broiled steaks."

The New Medical School and University Hospital in Ulm

Early in 1980, when I was a guest speaker for the European Society of Nuclear Medicine in Wiesbaden, Germany, the society sent five of us heads of nuclear medicine on a bus tour of nuclear medicine facilities in some of the cities of Germany. The last evening was in Ulm. A professor of medicine who was chairman of the department of internal medicine there at the university took us on a tour through their completely brand new medical school and university hospital. At about ten o'clock we settled down in a classroom for any questions. I asked him where they had received the money for this incredibly beautiful, complete medical school. He said that I probably had never heard of the source. I said, "Try me." They said that it was built by the Florence Schust Knoll Bassett Foundation.

My first sentence in my introduction to my first date (in the eighth grade) is, "I constantly advise our grandchildren to never underestimate any child in their school and classes." I have now illustrated from my own experience the effects of Charlie Christie, my seventh-grade woodworking teacher, and of Eliel Saarinen, the famous, internationally known architect.

Tenth Grade

Football Practice

In his pleasant and reasonable but firm way, my father convinced me that I must turn out for football in the tenth grade. He believed that I was spending too many hours thinking and reading about scientific things and not enough time in athletics. I was five foot 6 inches tall and weighed 115 pounds.

I had never played football and was not interested. As a result of turning out for football, however, two very important events touched my life in the tenth grade.

Accidental Death of Two of My Friends

The people who had turned out for football practice walked about one mile from Saginaw High School to the football field every evening. I would inevitably get into intense conversations with one of my best friends during this walk. I was in just such a conversation with one of my best friends when our friend, Bill Draper, en route to the football field in his Cadillac limousine (*full of boys*) stopped at our curb to ask if we wanted a ride to the field. We almost routinely accepted these generous gestures and stood on the running boards of the cars holding on through an open window. The only reason we refused the ride that evening, after some thought, was we were in the middle of a very exciting and intimate conversation.

Two of my best friends, Bernie Schneider and Franny Shrems, were walking thirty feet ahead of us. Bill Draper stopped and offered them a ride and they accepted. The street curved to the left about three blocks ahead of us, and they were both standing on the same running board on the right side of

30

the car. When Bill Draper started turning to the left to round the curve, the car leaned unusually far to the right and was perilously close to the curb. One of our friends was crushed to death by a telephone post at the curb and the second was fatally injured when the pole knocked him off the car and into an adjacent tree.

This was my first striking source of salvation by "the everlasting grace" that miraculously saved my life many times when death had a high statistical probability of ending my career. To this day, I look upon that incident as a "miracle."

Elected Class President

An intelligent and dedicated young classmate of mine, who became president of our class in the eleventh and twelfth grades and made it a career of hers, first ran for this position in the tenth grade. She would have been a "shoo-in" for this job, had it not been for the fact that approximately 361 boys had turned out for football. They had found me nonthreatening to their football careers and quite jovial when they saw I was there at the request of my father and had a good sense of humor about the whole thing and was determined to enjoy them and our football practices.

I also had the maximum growth spurt of my life that year and grew two and a half inches and gained fifteen pounds during that semester. They decided that, since I was the only one out for football who was willing to be class president, they would all campaign and vote for me. As you will see later, this presidency was to be followed by other presidencies in scientific societies and I learned a lot.

The Ultimate Race—
Before, During, and After

Before

History of This Unique Race

Bill Robinson, assistant editor of *Yachting* magazine in 1960, said it all in his introduction to the book, *A Berth to Bermuda* (his account of the 1960 Bermuda race), when he said:

> In the world of yachting, a very few events have come, over the years, to symbolize the best there is in the sport. For those who race big machines around buoys in the span of one day, the America's Cup is the Holy Grail and small boat skippers have made an Olympic berth their shining goal, but to the special breed whose eyes turn offshore, who go to sea and live in and with the boat for days and nights on end, there is nothing to match the glamour and prestige, the final challenge of the Bermuda Race.
>
> There are other big ones. England has the Fastnet, the West Coast its long tradewind sleigh ride to Honolulu, and Great Lakes sailors come back again and again to the two races to Mackinaw. Now and then, a transatlantic race causes a stir, but to captains and crews in all of them, there comes the feeling at some time or other that they haven't been in the big one until they have sailed to Bermuda. The Bermuda Race has everything for the offshore sailor. It starts at Newport, R.I., in surroundings steeped in New England's maritime history and crosses one of the most varied, challenging stretches of ocean in the world. From the cold foggy seas of the coast, across the ever mysterious Gulf Stream and its area of violent changes, to the warm blue waters south of it, it is a 635-mile kaleidoscope of all the ocean's moods with the bright lure of Bermuda's pink coral and oleander-scented beauty as a reward at its end.

In the June 1976 issue of *Yachting*, Carleton Mitchell made the following statement about the 1960 race to Bermuda:

The 1960 race to Bermuda has been well chronicled, also undoubtedly lingers in the memory of anyone who sailed it. After light reaching and running breezes beyond the Gulf Stream, a real "buster" swept the fleet. There were knock-downs and a dismasting. Some boats hove to under trisail, others lay ahull with bare poles, a few even ran off dragging lines astern. Hurricane-strength gusts were recorded aboard one large vessel carrying an anemometer and most experienced seamen agreed there was a sustained gale of force 8-9.

In a description of the 1972 Newport-to-Bermuda race in the August issue of *Yachting*, Mitchell stated that one boat "had to battle through a storm near the finish that, while not as severe at its top limits as the 1960 one, was all that anyone racing offshore in a sailboat would ever care to meet."

Alf Loomis, in his foreword to *A Berth to Bermuda*, states:

There were 135 yachts participating in the Bermuda race which is the 22nd of a long series. Approximately 1,144 persons were aboard them. It was the largest armada of pleasure craft that had ever assembled for an event of this importance—635 miles through the cool waters of the Continental Shelf, across the hot rushing current of the Gulf Stream, and beyond to a haven among the tiny islands of Bermuda.

The 72-foot ketch *Barlovento II* was one of the largest of the five classes and had been broken in on smaller races the year before. The 58-foot yawl, *Ondine*, owned by Huey Long, was so new the workmen from the yard in which she was built were bundled off her deck less than 48 hours before the race began. The smallest starter was a new sloop from Sweden, the 32-foot *Casella* with a crew of only four.

Then there were old yachts which had been there before whose names are known to every ocean racing scoundrel. For example, the schooner *Nina*. She had won a race to Spain in 1928—the first transatlantic event for small craft and had participated in seven Bermuda races since the close of World War II.[1] The yawl *Stormy Weather* had been five times to Bermuda and had won the transatlantic race to Norway in 1935 and had topped off her record by winning that same year the Fastnet premiere

1. Please see that this is the fulfilled prophecy of Charlie Christie.

British ocean race. The ketch *Malibar XIII*, four times a contestant in the Bermuda race, had been dismasted at the start of the Fastnet race of 1951 but not until after she had won the longest ocean race ever sailed, that of 4,000 miles from Havana to San Sebastian, Spain.

The cutter *Nimrod V*, a frequent competitor in the Bermuda race, had in 1939 under her original name of *Blitzen* won the long race which that year was sailed from San Francisco to Honolulu. *White Mist*, an invariable participant since her construction in 1950, had, though racing in the smallest class, been first to finish in 1953 in the 1,200-mile windward race from Buenos Aires to Rio de Janeiro. Four years later, she won in her class in still another race to Spain. The cutter *Highland Light*, third to finish and place in the transatlantic race to England in 1931, had in 1932 set a record for the Bermuda course which was not eclipsed for 24 years. Since the war, the *Light* has never failed to carry the Navy's colors to Bermuda.

Here in the fleet at the foggy start was *Carina*, unique in being the only yacht to have won two transatlantic races, to Sweden in 1955 and to Spain in 1957, and to have followed through to victory in the succeeding Fastnets. Previous winners of the Bermuda race were likewise represented—the *Gesture* of 1946, the *Argyll* of 1950, and the original *Carina* of 1952—now *CheeChee V*. Last, but by no means least in this brilliant galaxy, there was *Finisterre*, which in 1958 had crowned her startling victory of 1956 and was destined to sail phenomenally on and do it again in 1900.

From foreign lands—Argentina, Brazil, Bermuda and Canada (which aren't very foreign), Germany, Great Britain, and Sweden—came 15 yachts. Of these, the British sloop *Belmore*, sailed by the Royal Navy under Commander Errol Bruce of the Royal Navy Sailing Association, was to come closer to victory than any visitor from overseas has ever done. Only *Finisterre* and a margin of 25 minutes separated *Belmore* from the major honors.

These historic yachts and their accomplishments are cited here to indicate the quality of the fleet. It made me proud to see in *A Berth to Bermuda* that we were in Class D, the next to the smallest boats. *Siskiwit* was owned by my closest friend and medical fraternity brother, John Pierpont, from the Upper Peninsula of Michigan. We ended in the fleet position 103 out of 135 boats. No time was available on three boats, and one boat in our class was disabled and one dismasted. One other boat in Class E was also dismasted.

Childhood Preparation

My preparation for the race was actually started by my father renting a cottage in Sebewaing on Saginaw Bay. We have pictures of me at a dock there in a big rowboat trying to row when I was four years of age. My mother and father had been members of the "Saginaw Canoe Club." They and their friends also sailed these canoes with a lateen rig.

Our cottage at Killarney was on an all-sand beach with five sand bars. Our childhood activities were restricted in a graduated fashion from sand bar number one near shore to sand bar number five, farthest from the shore.

When we had a "northeaster" (strong wind blowing straight in) and it caused waves up to four feet high, there would be breakers up to six feet high on the outermost sand bar. My father acquired a beautiful sixteen-foot rowing boat, Clinker built, the *Georgianna*, from D. D. Buick—of the Buick automobile family. It had four oarlocks and oars and a special seat for the helmsman. It also had brass handrails on the bow and stern! After we had learned how to swim at about six or seven years of age, we learned to row out into a northeaster to see if we could successfully row through all the waves without sinking. If we made it out past all the sand bars, the next quest was to turn around and see if we could row back in through the cascading breakers without sinking.

By about age ten years, we loved to spend practically all day long rowing out through breakers as high as six feet.

In the peak of the Bermuda "buster," the seventy-two-foot yawl *Barlovento* recorded on its electrical wind anemometer wind velocities never less than sixty knots for five hours and exceeding eighty knots several times. Eighty knots was as high as the anemometer recorded.[2]

2. Small craft advisory = winds up to 33 knots; gale = winds of 34–47 knots, storm = winds of 48–63 knots; hurricane = winds of 64 knots and above. *Chapman Piloting*, 59th Edition, Elbert S. Maloney, (New York: Hearst Marine Books, 1989).

The United States and British destroyers accompanying the race recorded maximum sea heights averaging thirty feet, with six-foot breakers commonly on the tops of these waves. The waves were about five hundred feet from trough to crest in length and, of course, looked like they were five hundred feet high.

I was the only person on the *Siskiwit* who had directly experienced six-foot breakers repeatedly. It was of interest to me that most of the crew's anxiety was caused by the loud "crash" of the breakers on our cabin top. Another reason I was not panicked by the six-foot breaker crashes on the cabin top was that the boat had just been reconditioned under ideal circumstances.

Preparation of the Siskiwit

In the four years of our sailing together in two Mackinaw races a year (one about 175 miles in length and the other 270 miles in length), I had only missed one Chicago-Mackinaw race and the boat was dismasted in the race during a spinnaker run.

John Pierpont, our owner and skipper, had Sparkman and Stevens (the most famous United States naval architects at that time) redesign our standing rigging. John then had the most famous shipyards on the Great Lakes (Palmer Johnson on Lake Michigan) recaulk the deck and rebuild the new standing rigging.

The boat, though made of mahogany, had every other rib inside the hull made of steel. It had bent white oak frames every six inches inside the cabin top.

Requirements for Admission

Also of great importance is that the Newport-to-Bermuda race committee (in the National Yachting Association) had excellent safety requirements for all boats and crews.

All boats were required to have bow and stern pulpits and

lifelines around the sides of the boat attached to these pulpits. All boats were required to have a storm jib and a storm trisail as well as reefing capabilities of the mainsail. All boats were also required to have assorted jibs of the appropriate strengths of sailcloth, depending upon the size of the sail.

Perhaps most important was that at least four members of the crew must have raced in at least one long distance, overnight race of not less than 150 miles every year for two years. We had six members out of eight who had raced in the 175-mile Port Huron-Mackinaw and the 270-mile Chicago-Mackinaw race every year for four years.

In addition, the Bermuda race committee required that the skipper had to have one member who was qualified to do celestial navigation. Our skipper, John Pierpont, who was also the owner, had one of our men, Jeff Pope, officially trained by the United States Coast Guard in celestial navigation for one year.

In addition, I purchased a sextant with an instruction book and all the tables and took my sextant with me to all the scientific lectures and meetings I had to attend as part of my job. I practiced primarily sunrises and sunsets and stars. Thank heavens Jeff proved to be an excellent navigator. I checked his shots day and night primarily for my education and also to be certain we had an auxiliary navigator in case Jeff became incapacitated or was lost overnight or killed by a flying boom (the most common cause of death on a sailboat). I had been the first mate and official navigator when we moved the boat from the Apostle Islands in the western end of Lake Superior down to Port Huron in the lower end of Lake Huron and the Mackinaw races.

I had also been impressed that Carleton Mitchell, who had already won two Newport-to-Bermuda races in a row in his boat, the *Finisterre*, allegedly required that everyone on the boat ate a meal at 7:00 A.M., 12:00 noon and 6:00 P.M. He also believed very strongly that everyone should be resting when they were not on watch. Allegedly, he insisted that they lie on their bunks with eyeshades on and earplugs whenever they were not on watch to make certain that they had the maximum rest. I had strongly encouraged that practice in the Mackinaw races and also in the Newport-to-Bermuda race.

We had also had a couple of spinnaker knockdowns[3] with the companionways open and once came up with about two feet of water over the floorboards. I therefore wrote an acceptance letter to the skipper for the Newport-to-Bermuda race that strongly requested that anytime we had the spinnaker up we have the hatches closed. Each of us was also required to have a lifeline that attached from our belt to a rail or any reliable fitting on the boat to hold us in the boat regardless of what we were doing with our hands and feet when we were in strong winds and big waves, *especially* at night!

Fortunately, I had also experienced two "white line squalls"[4] in the Great Lakes. These are sudden, very strong bursts of wind that occur in the presence of a clear sky without any visible warning. When I saw one of these coming across the ocean in the Bermuda race, I told the skipper that the water looked like a white line squall and he promptly demanded that we drop the spinnaker and all the sail instantly, which we did.

The day before the race to Bermuda, I spent considerable time worrying about and thinking about what we should do if we got into a real buster since we had never experienced a wind on the Great Lakes of over forty-five or fifty miles an hour, except for a couple of short winds pushing at seventy knots. We also thought up the simplest possible way to do celestial navigation so that it could be done on a tossing boat under adverse circumstances when we were very tired.

Newport, Rhode Island, before the Race

I have presented a brief synopsis of published articles on this race in the introduction above.

---

3. The top of the mast may hit the water and the rudder rises out of the water!
4. These are also known as "shear lines" that create dangerous conditions for aircraft during takeoff and/or landing.

Newport, already a busy yachting center and naval port that teems with sailors in shoregoing whites, had the atmosphere of a college town on the morning of a big football game. There was an electric expectancy in the air as the tempo of last-minute activity stepped up hour by hour. By car, bus, and plane, crews poured in, duffle bags on shoulder, to join boats brought in by owners, paid hands, and skeleton crews.

Friday night, June 17, 1960, found the town bursting at the seams and the harbor a floating boat show the like of which had never been seen before. Last-minute instructions were handed out at the captain's meeting and all hands repaired to the Viking Hotel for a mammoth cocktail party that filled the hotel garden with teeming humanity. Wives, smiling, nervous, and hiding anxiety, put a brave face on the final festivities as the gaiety mounted to a fitful peak. Fog settled over Newport like a thick wet blanket.

The next morning, June 18, 1960, the fog was thicker than ever, and fog and tension hung over the anchorage in equal parts. There was even talk that the start might be postponed. The crew was kept busy with last-minute gear checks and stowage. We headed blindly for the deep shut-in row of Brenton Reef light vessel and finally came up to her in the murk. How could we ever start in this? The other end of the line was hidden completely as we groped our way past an anchored freighter and finally the committee boat. Postponement was signalled as we came alongside. What next? Imagine the anti-climax of heading back into Newport.

As we were heading for the starting line in the fog, I was down in the cabin getting lunch for the eight of us. I suddenly became aware of the fact that the principal difference between the Great Lakes and the ocean is that the ocean is much deeper than the Great Lakes so that the waves are longer but not as high for the same wind and fetch. Second, the waves on the Great Lakes are almost always current with the wind while the waves on the ocean are a combination of "yesterday's" wind and "today's" wind, thus causing waves from two different directions. I decided to climb out of the cabin and look at the horizon to quiet down my stomach. Much to my surprise, there was Carleton Mitchell's *Finisterre* (#260) on the sail. I got an excellent picture of her near us with my camera. It was amusing to me that she was in Class E (the smallest boats). We were in Class D and yet we were approximately the same length. The principal difference was that she was not as heavy as ours because she had a centerboard through the keel while we had just a deep long keel. She was obviously the number one boat to beat because she had already won the 1956 and 1958 Bermuda races and had practically the same crew. The other impression I have was of seeing the *Ondine* (#281) owned by "Huey" Long. It was so new that they were still working on getting it ready during the preparation for the start of the race. I also was impressed to see the *Dyna* (A, 7), which was a huge aluminum yawl that had been the most successful boat in the Mackinaw races.

Visibility improved and suddenly we got what we thought was a warning signal from the committee boat, though her bridge was hidden. Class A started first with the first gun.

During

One of the first boats in the starting area was *Nina*, a grand old lady of the sport, one of the few schooners still in top-flight competition. Built in 1928, she gleamed like new in the slanting light. I have referred to Charlie Christie's interest in the *Nina*, and my brother had built a sailing model of this influenced by the prediction that it would turn out to be one of the great racing sailboats of all time.

The start in a moderate southerly was close and exciting. All eyes were on the committee boat as Class A bore down on the line and the big boats jammed up like bluejays in a Sunday regatta. Unfortunately, it was one of the few excitements of a two-hundred-mile drifter.

After the rush and confusion of the start, there was very little sense of being in a race. Within minutes, the fleet went off into the fog and each boat was left in lonely isolation, close hauled on the starboard tack on its two-hundred-yard square patch of foggy ocean. Pale light filtered from overhead, though the most errant optimist would have been hard pressed to call it sunshine, and the breeze built to a respectful ten to twelve knots.

The basic strategy in the Bermuda course is classic and is very seldom tampered with by experienced Bermuda hands. The doctrine is to hold as high as possible to the west of the rhumb line—the direct Newport-to-Bermuda course—in order to have as much westing under the keel as possible when entering the Gulf Stream a third of the way on the route. In this way, the easterly set of the stream will carry the boat only back to the rhumb line, not east of it where she would be too far to leeward of the island in the southwest breezes that usually prevail on approach to it.

The added complication in crossing the Gulf Stream, however, is that it seldom runs in a straight course. It meanders along in looping curves. Everyone tries to head for it. Upon nearing it, a constant check of water temperature is the best help in finding the meander and all boats are equipped with portable and built-in water thermometers.

June 19, 1960, the Calm

On Sunday, the second day, the spinnaker breeze failed and the wind came light ahead. We had seen only schools of porpoises, and at night an occasional flying fish had come aboard.

June 20, 1960, the Calm

We spent most of the third day a hundred yards behind another boat, looking down into the cockpit from behind without another boat visible.

On a spinnaker reach in the sun, I suddenly realized that the windward spinnaker sheet was reaved through a five-pound brass snatch block. It occurred to me that, if the snatch block was screwed onto the deck instead of being bolted through-and-through, it might suddenly pull out and aim directly for my head at about sixty miles an hour. I changed my position so that this blow to my head could not happen. Five minutes later I heard a sound like an arrow shot out of a bow string. The snatch block had disappeared at a great speed off into space, and the spinnaker jolted from the sudden laxity of the sheet. The skipper immediately bolted on the other snatch block.

We took the temperature of the water at thirty-minute intervals, and it suddenly rose from 63° to 73°. We had suddenly entered the Gulf Stream 30 to 50 miles west of the rhumb line (149° the rhumb line was 162° magnetic).

June 21, 1960, the Calm

On Tuesday, the fourth day, we awakened to almost no breeze in the morning. The wind picked up in the evening. In

45

my diary it is recorded that we sighted seaweed, a school of twenty porpoises, and Portuguese man-of-war, and a six-foot-diameter ocean turtle that day.

June 22, 1960, the "Buster" Develops Slowly

On the fifth day, Wednesday, we found ourselves surrounded by black clouds with rain and winds from the southwest. We were close hauled. In the afternoon we gradually had to take two reefs in the main and change to the #2 *Genoa*. There was no change in the barometer. I started my watch as watch captain and first mate with three men at eight o'clock in the evening under the #2 *Genoa* with the main dropped and furled. We found ourselves in a wild beat in constantly increasing wind and waves and the rainfall became torrential.

What disturbed me most as the evening progressed, besides the constantly increasing wind velocity, was the beginning of wide shifts in the direction and velocity of the wind. As we got down to a maximum reefed main and the smallest jib short of the storm jib, I decided the best place for me was up forward on the cabin top with my back to the mast fastened on with a steel line to shout at the crew about the wide wind shifts to be certain that we did not get the wind on the wrong side of the main and *Genoa*.

We read later that the big Navy yawl during this time had at least six men on the windward rail with their bodies securely fastened by steel lifelines to the rail so that they would not fall overboard. One wind shift caught the *Genoa* and the main on the wrong side, and the rail went so far underwater that they found themselves held underwater by their lifelines. One of the crew related that he said to himself that he obviously had to let his lifeline go to keep from being drowned. It then occurred to him that if he let the lifeline go, where would he be then? He was pleased that he decided to hold on a few seconds more because suddenly the wind made another violent shift and their rail was up in the air again.

At 11:45 P.M., we had to drop jib and put up the storm tri-sail. Later, my crew got a great kick out of the fact that their

46

first mate and watch captain, Bill Beierwaltes, was holding desperately onto the rail while steering with the tiller and screaming orders at the other three men on how they could drop the jib and put up the storm trisail. I am certain that at least one of the eighty-plus-mile-an-hour puffs hit us after we had gotten all the sail off and we seriously considered not putting up any sail at all.

The Buster

The storm trisail worked fine and, by this time, it was twelve o'clock at night and the rain simulated Niagara Falls. I had never seen so much water fall in such a short space of time. Nevertheless, I knew that, if we wanted to win, we would have to put up the storm jib. I yelled at the crew to do so, but John Pierpont, the skipper, was obviously awake below and pounded on the deck to let me know that he did not want the storm jib put up. It occurred to me why he didn't. The sail hatch was halfway back on the forward deck from the bow to the mast. It would have been easy for someone to be washed overboard by the six-foot breakers on thirty-foot seas. It also would have been easy for the hatch cover to wash overboard or be blown overboard. It also would have been easy for a six-foot breaker to come down through the forward hatch and fill the boat.

I went below and told the skipper that it was twelve o'clock and our watch was over and asked him to get his watch up. None of his watch would come up, but Lyman Bittman from my watch said he would stay up with the skipper. I asked him why and he said that he wanted to be up on deck because he wasn't going to go down with the ship and drown. I said, "Lyman, the depth here is five and a half miles and you're more than one hundred miles from shore. It really doesn't matter whether you're sleeping inside the boat or you're on the deck when the boat goes down." We were, of course, required to carry an inflatable life raft on the deck for just such an emergency. It then occurred to me that, if we inflated the life raft in an eighty-mile-an-hour wind, it would be blown off to sea. It is also difficult to see how eight men could get into a life raft when the boat was on its beam end in thirty-foot seas with six-foot breakers.

The *Escapade* reported hearing on their radio that first one, then two, then three boats were dismasted as their anemometer recorded a wind of over forty-five knots. Three rudders were lost. Many boats developed bad leaks and bilge pumps became jammed with paper labels, etc. There were numerous SOSs and the Coast Guard brought in three boats. The *Concordia* yawl lost its main masthead while up with the *Finisterre*.

At any rate, I slept in an upper pipe berth and, as I lay down to sleep, there was a constant dripping of water on my face. I realized, however, that the temperature of the water was 84 degrees and that it was much more comfortable here than it was on deck. I also realized that, as soon as I could relax, I would sleep very soundly.

Lyman Bittman and John Pierpont stayed in the cockpit from twelve at night until four in the morning. It should be remembered that every six-foot breaker, which occurred roughly on the top of every twentieth sea, instantly filled the cockpit. All long distance racing boats are required by the Cruising Club of America to have cockpits small enough and with large enough standard drains so that the breaking wave will not smash the cockpit and so that it will empty quickly before the next wave.

June 23, 1960

By four o'clock that morning, the rain had stopped and the wind shifts had returned to regular smaller shifts. The wind had also dropped to between forty and fifty knots. I relieved the skipper and Lyman and got two of the skipper's sons and Jeff, our navigator, to come up on deck and get things going again. The first thing we did was put up the #2 jib.

The seas were awesome. Every sea was like the first hill on a roller coaster. We would literally gasp for breath and have a frozen grimace on our face and white knuckles. We would then start to breathe again and relax a little before the next sea came down on us. As dawn started, I was able to get a picture of one good sea. I noticed in *A Berth to Bermuda* that there is an almost identical picture on page 94. Also, on page 94, it is stated that on the *Barlovento* at 2200 a puff of wind sent the needle on the anemometer up to 60 and that for the rest of the night the anemometer stayed in the 60s while the crew stayed in a world of blackness and hideous sound. It seems to me that the most frightening thing is the shriek of wind through the rigging that convinces you that the rigging is going to be blown off into the sea. They stated that the anemometer needle never went below 60 for the whole period of 0400–0500 wheel trick and twice they watched it "spurt to the top of the dial past 80 as the first blast of a gust hit them tearing off the tops of the waves that reared over them and blowing them straight up." There is another beautiful picture of one of these waves on page 98.

I learned later that the crew of the *Finisterre* drove their boat hard through the storm with at least the small mizzen and a storm jib. It is believed that this may be one of the major reasons that she was thirteen hours shorter in lapsed time than we were.

As the seas were building up and the breakers rose in height, there was a discussion on our boat as to whether we should heave to or run for it or use a sea anchor. I reminded them that I had taken *Yachting* since I was a child and had settled this question a long time ago. To me, the most horrible experience would be pitch polling. Here the boat rides forward on a very high wave as the bow goes under until finally the boat turns over end for end with the masts pointing directly to the bottom of the ocean. The second most horrible experience that some have had is to have the boat roll over sideways 360 degrees. Needless to say, both of these result in loss of the body or multiple fractures with the body fastened securely to the boat with a steel line.

On the other hand, everyone who has hove to feels better. (The wind drawing on a storm trisail located in the proper lee side of the boat with the storm jib back to windward to keep the boat from coming up into the wind and turning off on the opposite tack.) The boat is going neither forward nor backward but sideways at a modest rate of speed, and the sails keep the boat from rocking as violently from side to side and make the motion of the boat much smoother.

49

One of the statements made about the *Finisterre* was that it was driving sufficiently on a close reach with sailpower to "porpoise." I experienced this a few years after the Bermuda race in a Port Huron-to-Mackinaw race outside of Saginaw Bay in Lake Huron when the wind was about twenty-five knots and the seas were about eight feet high and about forty feet from trough to crest. The bow of the boat tends to shoot up in the air as the boat is carried somewhat out of the water. The wind pushing sideways on the sails makes the boat turn on its side so that the mast tends to become parallel with the water with the boat modestly up in the air. The boat then crashes downward on its side in the next sea, creating a dramatic crashing experience.

The reason I didn't want to take off the sails and put on a sea anchor was that, if a big boat goes backward rapidly and fairly dramatically from a six-foot breaker on a thirty-foot sea, the rudder is thrown sideways under great pressure against the transom and the rudder may break off. We later learned that rudders had been broken off many boats and boats had become dismasted due to rigging failure.

As the storm abated, I asked Jeff to do his best navigation possible that night so that, when we saw lights from a freighter or the destroyers, we would not think, *This might be Bermuda.* We did see lights and were glad that we felt confident of our navigation.

June 24, 1960, Bermuda

On Friday we sighted Bermuda at 9:30 in the morning. We were thirteen miles east of Bermuda. We had a nice breeze on a close reach, and by noon we were approaching Bermuda. I stupidly changed into shorts and a short-sleeve shirt and developed a blistering sunburn.

We wanted to make a perfect finish across the finish line in front of the judges with the #1 *Genoa* and the full main up. As soon as we rounded the line, we came about and got a "rap" of the *Genoa* sheet caught on the largest winch so that we could not free it. We actually had to take a knife and cut the sheet free to finish the race. I am certain that the race committee said,

"How in the world can these poor devils have negotiated that terrible buster successfully when they can't even round the finish line in a nice wind?" As we approached the Royal Bermuda Yacht Club, the *Finisterre* was in the honorary position of the winner.

When we had anchored, the Royal Bermuda Yacht Club tender came up to take us to shore with crews from other boats. They asked us if we knew that during the peak of the storm a crew member of one of the boats had fallen off and was later rescued. They told us that, if we wanted to meet the man, we should take the road from the yacht club directly into town where on the main street we could find him "beating the hell out of the drums" in the Salvation Army band.

Thoughts after the Race

Man Overboard

The race and the story of the one man falling overboard appeared later in *Sports Illustrated* and just about every boating and yachting magazine, etc. The book, *A Berth to Bermuda*, says that the "man overboard" occurred on the *Scylla*. Jack Weston was recovered forty minutes after being swept overboard. The *Scylla* was in Class E, the smallest boats, and her skipper was Charles Ulmer; they were listed as being in fleet position 10. Ulmer was also a famous sailmaker.

The story was that, as the crew boarded the boat for the race, one of them gave the skipper a battery for the boat. When the skipper asked why, the crewman answered that they always finished races without any electrical power and he wanted to be sure they had it this time. A second crewman gave another present to the skipper, which was a brand-new stroboscopic light that could be attached to the horseshoe life preserver, commonly attached to the rear pulpit of the boat to be thrown over when a crew member fell overboard. The story was that the crew member was already standing down in the companionway through the back of the cabin when the boat porpoised and threw him out of the boat into the water. The articles quoted him as saying that as he went under water, "a deep sense of loneliness came over me."

At first, he thought he was permanently lost and he became disturbed. He found that he was unable to see anything with his head above water. Suddenly, as a wave crashed over his head, with his eyes open, he could see a light. Again, he could not see the light with his head above water, so he opened his eyes and put his head under water and again found the light. He therefore swam in that direction. He said that at last he felt that there was hope when he was able to rest his body on the horseshoe life preserver with the stroboscopic light flashing.

In the meantime, the article said, the crew did everything right. One man kept his eye on the man where he had fallen overboard while another one threw in the life preserver with the stroboscopic light on it and the skipper recorded the course and the line of position. An immediate attempt was made to come about under sail. When this failed, the engine was tried and the battery was obviously dead. The skipper then went forward under unbelievably difficult conditions and got the new battery and installed it. At last, the motor worked and they were able to come about. They then were able to rescue the man within forty minutes of his falling overboard. He no longer had to work as a crew member because he was too frightened by his dreadful experience.

As we got off the launch and went ashore at the Royal Bermuda Yacht Club, I confirmed permanently what I had suspected earlier. I had never been seasick, but when I walked on shore, I could hardly stand up and even became mildly nauseated. The people who had felt modestly seasick and nauseated on the boat immediately felt good when they went ashore.

Carleton Mitchell

Later, stories poured in about the winner, Carleton Mitchell and the *Finisterre*. The press had converged upon Carleton Mitchell. They said, "Mr. Mitchell, no one has ever won even two Bermuda races in a row and you have now won your third Bermuda race in a row. The strong conviction that everyone has is that you will go down as the most famous ocean yacht racer in the world because your feat will never be carried out again. Do you have any explanation for such an incredible accomplishment?"

Carleton Mitchell answered that yes, he believed he did know the answer. He stated, "I have raced in most of the great ocean races for twenty-five years and I believe that I have made just about every mistake that is possible to make. If I have done something differently than others, it is that I have taken each mistake very seriously. I have sat down with a notebook and pen and written down the mistake and then thought through how I could prevent this mistake from ever happening again."

I have used this story repeatedly with employees and children as a wonderful philosophy of life. It reassures the person who has made the mistake that it is normal to make mistakes and the people should not feel badly about them as long as they sit down and think long and seriously about the mistake and how they could avoid ever making this mistake again.

The other big effect that this race had on me was that I realized we had successfully got the boat out there from the west end of Lake Superior and back again without a single serious mishap. We had also done everything right and in a scientific fashion step by step as the wind increased to over eighty knots and the seas rose to thirty feet high with six-foot breakers. Although we came in thirteen hours after the winner, we were in position 103 out of 135 boats, most of which had raced regularly in numerous ocean races with far more money, professional skippers, etc. I therefore decided that I had nothing to fear in sailing in the future and that it could all be done in a scientific fashion.

At age seventy-seven, it has occurred to me that this has proven to be true and it is very reassuring. It is also clear to me that Carleton Mitchell had the money and the brains to engage a naval architect to make an entirely different type of boat that was particularly good for the Newport-to-Bermuda race conditions. The previous boats had deep heavy hulls with long keels. Mitchell's boat was much lighter and depended on its wide beam for stability. In light airs and in reaches, he could pull up the centerboard to various heights as we had always done in sailing dinghies on Barton Pond. Let us say that his boat was one of the first steps in the theory that the fastest boats would be like a sailing dinghy with the concept that "light is fast" and also that you should not have anything dragging in the water that you don't have to have for the particular wind strength and its direction. Even the around-the-world Whitbred race maxies today and the new sixty-footers simulate racing dinghies in that they have a low freeboard and are extremely light.

It has been stated that, when the wind rises above thirty

knots, everyone starts pumping adrenaline out of his or her adrenal medulla to cause a certain amount of anxiety. Needless to say, when the wind hits eighty knots or over, there is a maximum secretion of adrenaline.

It was of interest to me what thoughts attacked me during the time of the buster. The first thought was that I was scheduled to go to England to my first International Thyroid Association meeting in London. I also had made arrangements to take my wife and my father with me and to take our children to my wife's sister in Amherst.

I told several people that I didn't mind a little storm as long as I knew how long the storm would last.

Shipmates reassured me every time I brought up this subject that they couldn't care less about my appointments and commitments to airlines and hotels; all they were interested in was surviving the immediate incident. If I had consulted the proper navigational tables under that time of year and in that location, I would have learned that winds above sixty knots last an average time period of less than twenty-four hours. Again, more scientific knowledge would have prevented that thought.

The second thought that dominated my thinking throughout the big wave experience was of how I could tell our children and grandchildren and friends how big the waves and the breakers actually were and how strong the wind was. I was sure that their thought would only be that I was an old blowhard prone to exaggeration. I was therefore delighted when Robinson wrote the first book on this race titled, *A Berth to Bermuda*. My final questions were put to rest in August of 1972 when I read the article in *Yachting* on the latest buster. This is the paragraph that stated that "although the boats had to battle through a storm near the finish, that, while not as severe at its top limits as the 1960 one, the storm was all that anyone racing offshore in a sailboat would ever care to meet."

I decided that, if they could read that plus my brief scientific description in my book showing that the winds had reached hurricane strength and not believe the evidence, there was no point in talking to them.

It is of interest to me that three months after I had finished the race, the chairman of my Department of Internal Medicine with whom I was having lunch, told me that he had the distinct feeling that I had never really gotten over the race and still became a little hypomanic whenever I discussed it. He asked me if that was true. I confessed that there was no question that was true.

It is also of interest to me that for a long time I was obsessed by trying to find pictorial expressions of what we had gone through. For example, thirty-four years later I still have a painting by Montague Dawson of two crew members on the side deck of a full-rigged ship with most of the sails furled plunging into a wave about thirty feet high with a six-foot breaker on top while at least a six-foot-high breaker is coming over the lee side of the boat as the crew members hold onto a lifeline on the side of the cabin to keep them from being washed overboard.

More Wind than the Fastnet Race

Lastly, the greatest damage in an ocean race of size was in the 1979 English Fastnet race through the Irish Sea. Fifteen sailors died, 26 boats were abandoned, and 194 racing boats retired from the race. Yet the wind in that race was not as strong as in the 1960 Bermuda race. The official statement about the Fastnet race is that a Beaufort Force 10 storm hit 303 starters. Chapman describes a Beaufort Force 10 as equalling forty-eight to fifty-five knots with waves of eighteen to thirty feet. A hurricane strength wind is sixty-four knots and over.

But the Fastnet race *did not require* boats to carry a storm jib or storm trisail. It did not require the crews to have raced together in a series of yearly long distance races. As a result, many of the boats that were abandoned were subsequently found floating and drifting about.

Medicine:
My Ultimate Contribution
(1938–1994)

Why Become a Physician?

Fear of Disease

My father passed on to me in conversations that ill health could strike you if you didn't obey certain folklore-transmitted concepts. For example, it was very important not to become chilled. One way to avoid chilling was to wear a cap or a hat when going out into cold air. Later, it was proved that a major source of heat loss is through one's scalp. He also impressed upon us the importance of going to bed at ten o'clock at night. There is now considerable evidence that, for maximum effectiveness in thinking, basically everyone requires eight hours of sleep. In a careful study of those who said they only needed four or six hours of sleep with or without naps, in studies of abstract thinking, mathematics, etc., it has now been pretty well documented that performance increases with up to eight hours of sleep a day.

There is also considerable evidence in the literature that an unusual fear of disease passed on to a child from, for example, a hypochondriacal parent is a common predecessor of people who become physicians. Presumably, he/she becomes a physician so that he/she will be able to keep up on what causes diseases, how to prevent them, and how to treat them in himself and his family.

I also remember my parents telling me not infrequently about an episode of severe whooping cough that I had when I was a very young child. The woman pediatrician attending me, Dr. Longstreet in Saginaw, made it clear to my mother that I would have to live or die by myself because every time I saw her, I screamed uncontrollably.

The Mystery of Sex

Another reason for going into medicine is to take the mystery out of sex and learn what one should or should not do about sex, qualitatively and quantitatively. While I was writing this, workers at the University of Chicago came out with the first definitive biostatistical study on this subject. It revealed that the Kinsey Report was the result of very poor, biased statistical methods of gathering information. The sexual wonders on television and in the media were obviously distorted to sell and earn money.

In the seventh grade, when my male classmates began to talk about their penile erections that embarrassed them when the teacher called upon them to get up and recite, they also began to talk more and more about the mysteries of sex. Indeed, it was either in the ninth or tenth grade that I was invited by four or five of my best friends to join them in one evening scheduled ahead of an activity that "blew my mind." One member of our social group in a Congregational church was a very attractive and provocative student one or two years behind us in school but obviously ahead of us in sexual development. I was told that she had volunteered to take on five of us simultaneously for intercourse one evening at her house when she knew her parents would be away.

Apparently, my mother's constant warnings much prior to this about the eventual horrors of causing an extramarital pregnancy and/or acquiring a sexually transmitted disease caused me to refuse this exciting invitation after considerable, somewhat disturbing forethought.

My mother also constantly warned me that young women were apt to become very emotional in the presence of certain young men and that it was up to the male sex to protect these young women from the dangers of extramarital sexual intercourse. Of course, my mother was never as explicit as I have put it above because she was afraid to talk to me about sex, and the mystery was vast and it was frustrating trying to learn the true facts.

I was totally ignorant about sex and had been thoroughly warned by my mother to not even talk about it. She was so disturbed by my handwork in the region of my penis when I was about twelve years of age that one noon, when my father and I were having lunch with her in our kitchen, she screamed at me in front of my father, "If you play with that thing once more, I'm going to cut it off with a butcher knife!" I started to cry uncontrollably, and my father gently but firmly interceded with my mother in front of me. He told her that we should both quiet down because my behavior was not abnormal and therefore it was inappropriate for my mother to yell at me, particularly because she would never dream of cutting off my penis with a knife and that I, of course, would try to be very careful not to use my hands like that in front of her.

My developing interest in all of the above certainly was in part caused by the new secretion of testosterone acting directly upon many appropriate tissues, including my cerebral cortex and upon my thinking.

In another area of interest, my best friend, Bill Baum, agreed with me that we should start picking up dead dogs, squirrels, etc., freshly killed on the streets of Saginaw by cars, and start dissecting them to see what the anatomy of life was all about.

Stan Crego's father was a dentist. He was easily encouraged to lend Bill and me a copy of his old *Gray's Human Anatomy*, and we subsequently spent many long hours together studying anatomy through the tenth and eleventh grades.

I had met Bill on a hike with some other boys. We then found out that our parents were old friends and the Baums also had a cottage and boats on Saginaw Bay at Point Lookout. Later, I encouraged Bill to leave Bay City Junior College to finish his premedical studies at the University of Michigan. I then encouraged him to join Phi Chi medical fraternity at the University of Michigan. He later became president of that fraternity.

Later, as I went into academic medicine as an internist, Bill interned and took his surgical residency and urology fellowship at the University of Michigan Hospital. After taking a professorship, he left Ann Arbor and started a very successful urological surgery private practice group in Muskegon for the rest of his medical career.

61

It also is of interest that he went into urology!

In college, I was most interested in embryology, particularly to learn about the sexual production of babies, their development in the uterus, and obstetrics. Only when I was taking junior-year internal medicine in medical school did a brilliant young internist lead me away from becoming an obstetrician and induced me to become a "medical detective"—an internist.

My First Biology Teacher

The *decision to become a physician*, however, was crystallized in the tenth grade (age fourteen years) by my biology teacher. In addition to the usual teaching, she introduced us to medical research. We were encouraged to bring our mothers' steam pressure cookers (very popular at that time for more rapidly preparing meals) to make a bacterial culture medium. We then planted the media with bacterial cultures furnished by our teacher and did experiments to show the relative potency of various biologicals in slowing the growth of these bacteria.

It is of interest that this is essentially the process used at least ten years later in the discovery of penicillin from a mold contaminating a bacterial culture.

In retrospect, I am very impressed by how tenth graders make such important career decisions. I remember one hour in one day making that career choice.

I decided that one should go into a specialty that was fun to learn, because the work of learning was obviously less work and more fun.

It was also obvious that, if one achieved straight As in that subject without thinking about it, one would be so highly motivated to learn it that he or she would enjoy spending far more hours and learn far more details and remember more details longer than if the motivation were weak or lacking.

I then reasoned, that afternoon, during that fateful one hour, that, now that the decision to become a biologist was made, I should decide what was the highest position to work toward in that field. First of all, I could be a high school biology teacher. What position was higher than that? Obviously, that would be a college biology professor. Was there anything higher than a college biology professor? I decided that the highest study in biology was man and that the physician learned most in this field.

I therefore, in one hour, reasoned through the choice of a career without any encouragement except by an "old" tenth-grade high school biology teacher just making her "routine" teaching interesting and challenging.

Books in the Eleventh Grade

In my eleventh grade year, Mrs. Mautner[1] gave me Valery Raydot's *The Life of Louis Pasteur* on December 24, 1934. I was thrilled by his work, discoveries, and applications of bacteriology for the betterment of millions of humans he would never see. I am positive that this had a powerful and stimulating influence on me and served as motivation for me to carry out forty-three years of successful research at the University of Michigan Medical School.

Grades in School

Although my parents both checked with me daily to be certain that I was conscientious about my homework and preparing for all scheduled examinations, I probably would not have achieved the grades to get into medical school, if it had not been for my brother and my girlfriend, Phyllis Sterling.

My brother was three years older than I. He was stimulated in his chemistry class in the tenth grade by Mrs. Fraker. When he started in chemistry at the University of Michigan, he had medical students as roommates in his rooming house during his first year at college. The message he transmitted to me was, "If you don't get straight As in biology, chemistry, and physics in high school, forget a career in medicine!"

1. Mrs. Mautner's husband was to later on in his will leave to my father his half interest in the Mautner and Krause Clothing Corporation

One lunch hour he was in the living room at our home in Saginaw at 904 Sheridan Avenue. He noticed that I was reading *Liberty* magazine. He asked me if I was about to take a physics exam. I said I was. He said, "Why don't you stop reading *Liberty* magazine and study for your physics examination until you leave home?"

Phyllis Sterling was my most compatible girlfriend in high school. She was delighted to find that I had decided to be a doctor. She asked me what my status was with the National Honor Society. I told her that I had never heard of it. She then explained the society to me and encouraged me to immediately put forth the effort to achieve the appropriate scholastic average to gain membership in the society because I was obviously bright enough to achieve membership easily. She was right, and I am most grateful to her for her interest. With these timely stimuli, I just noticed (1994) that I graduated magna cum laude from high school, fifteenth in my class.

I did apply for the one or two scholarships available through high school for college. They said that they preferred to award the scholarships based on need rather than academic achievement, and they said that I could not have a scholarship because my father earned enough money to put me through college. My father was such a legend in frugality that I did not learn that he was president of the Mautner and Krause Clothing Corporation and chairman of the board until he retired and the front page of the *Saginaw Daily News* totally informed my brother and me with full details and pictures of the officers of the corporation.

Interview with Dean Furstenberg

Someone urged me to visit with the dean of the University of Michigan Medical School in advance of starting the undergraduate program at the University of Michigan to see what I should take in my premedical program. I told my father. He said "Octy" Furstenberg was the dean of the medical school and he had played football with him in his high school years. I therefore scheduled an interview with Dr. Furstenberg and drove to Ann Arbor.

He asked me what my father and grandfather did. When he found that my paternal grandfather had a very successful meat market and ham-smoking establishment in Saginaw, he wondered if that career as a butcher made me interested in becoming a surgeon. (Dr. Furstenberg was practicing otorhinolaryngology and was reputed to have the highest earned income of any doctor in the state of Michigan.) I told him that the fact that my grandfather was a butcher may have encouraged me to think about becoming a physician, but I had not yet decided what subspecialty to enter. I told him that at the moment I was interested in the possibility of going into obstetrics and gynecology. Dr. Furstenberg told me two things: (1) If I held my grades to a *B+/A-* average and took a carefully constructed "combined" curriculum, I could obtain my Bachelor of Arts or Bachelor of Science degree at the end of my first four years with the award at the end of my first year of medical school. I would then obtain my M.D. degree three years later. I chose this curriculum because I wanted to get started being a doctor as soon as possible. (2) I should take only the required science courses in undergraduate school so that I would acquire the maximum general cultural college education before I started medical school. He stressed that once I started medical school nearly 100 percent of everything I read would be in medicine and science. I took his advice and, while not studying for my required courses and working board job, etc., I embarked on my own special reading program of Tolstoy, Dostoyevsky, Theater Guild Anthology, etc. I enjoyed acquiring this general cultural background immensely and am indebted to him for this first of his many good suggestions.

Jobs and Bicycle

Instead of joining an undergraduate social fraternity, I joined the Phi Chi medical fraternity in undergraduate school because I was working board job at Gamma Phi Beta sorority and two of the medical students ahead of me in Phi Chi were working board job there.

Because I had to be at board job frequently for breakfast

and always for lunch and dinner, and because my lectures and laboratories usually ended at noon, started again at 1:00 P.M. and finished at 5:00 P.M., I obviously had to have quick transportation. Students were not allowed to have cars. In 1934–35, I became known to many or most of my professors as "that student that rode a bicycle on the campus."

When I joined Phi Chi medical fraternity in 1937, I found that, if I could bicycle directly to the Rackham Graduate Building library or the law library or the main library on the campus, I could have totally preoccupied studying from the moment I got there until the library closed at either 10:30 or 11:00 at night.

My father made certain that I worked in his clothing store on Christmas vacations and whenever I was in Saginaw, unless I had a job elsewhere. He was particularly eager to have me become a nature study counselor at the YMCA camps, etc. rather than working at the Chevrolet foundry because this allowed me to continue my pleasures of swimming, sailing, and being outdoors.

The Chevrolet foundry paid much larger sums of money, but people were killed and injured there. I was promised a marvelous job at the Chevrolet foundry one December as an assistant to the doctor in charge to start the following June 15. He promised with great interest that he would teach me everything about the emergency room and first aid. When I got home on June 15 and reported to the foundry, the foundry was closed for the summer. As expected, I pounded the streets for two solid weeks before I got a job at the Heinz pickle factory, pushing pickles through a perforator. I came home thrilled because the official University of Michigan wage at that time was thirty-four cents an hour. The Heinz pickle factory paid me forty-three cents an hour, and *I was allowed to work twenty-three hours the first day there*! I soon found out why I was so lucky. My fingers were in the brine all day long, and I immediately started to lose my fingernails before I realized I would have to wear rubber gloves.

My Fascination with
the Thyroid Gland

My Mother

My parents were careful not to talk to Jack and me about the few illnesses that they had for fear we would worry about them. I never knew that in my college sophomore year my mother developed a goiter with thyrotoxicosis and had a surgical thyroidectomy to cure her. The thyrotoxicosis made her characteristically very nervous and shaky. After the thyroidectomy, she became severely hypothyroid and did not take her thyroid pills reliably. This led to her developing hypercholesterolemia, hypertension, and some tiny strokes before she finally had a big one and died at age seventy-six. This thyroid disease experience in my mother was my introduction to my lifelong interest in thyroid disease.

My Sister-in-Law

The second relevant event was when my brother's fiancée, Virginia Morgan, married Jack and they moved to Kalamazoo to begin their life in a new house. Virginia was very close to her mother, and Ginny immediately developed severe thyrotoxicosis because of threatened or actual separation from someone who was very close to her. I will never forget the drive that Jack, Ginny, and I had in his Model-A Ford from Kalamazoo to Saginaw while she was practically in the middle of a thyroid crisis. We stopped at every possible place during that one-hundred-mile drive to buy soft drinks and endless glasses of water to replace her massive fluid loss through sweating from the thyrotoxicosis. She also had a surgical thyroidectomy but took her thyroid replacement faithfully

In my junior year, I took an externship at Kalamazoo State Hospital with a close friend of mine from my class in medical school (who later went into surgery). I did research on depression that summer and developed a deep and permanent interest in psychiatry. My buddy and I also did autopsies on patients with wide-open pulmonary tuberculosis and splashed around tuberculous empyema fluid contamination. This proved to be the cause of my own tuberculosis that became evident halfway through my internship.

Junior-Year Autopsy of Thyroid Cancer

Also, in my junior year of medical school, I was assigned, as part of my routine work in my pathology course, an autopsy on a patient with thyroid cancer metastatic throughout her body. From then until the day I retired in 1994, thyroid cancer was my main obsession.

Senior Surgery Thesis on Thyroid Crisis

In my senior year of medical school, the head of surgery said that every senior student had to write a senior surgery thesis. He suggested to me that I might like to write on thyroid crisis since I had almost witnessed thyroid crisis while driving with my sister-in-law from Kalamazoo to Saginaw. I was delighted to do so.

World War II

When I started my internship at Cleveland City Hospital on July 1, 1941, my first senior attendant was perhaps the number one endocrinologist in Cleveland, Dr. Beard. Due to the fact that World War II had started and men and women were commonly separated from each other through the armed forces recruitment or through death on the battlefield, thyrotoxicosis (in the form of Graves' disease and, to a lesser extent, as Plummer's disease) was very common on my wards. My senior attendant, Dr. Beard, came to me one day and said, "I noticed that you are particularly interested in thyroid disease. I have a friend who is a professor in Boston named Ted Astwood who told me that he has a new pill that slows down the thyroid to get the patient ready for surgery and possibly may cure without surgery. This pill is called thiourea. Would you care to use it in our patients with thyrotoxicosis?" I said I would be delighted to use it and, before I went back to Ann Arbor in January 1944, I had written up twenty-seven patients whom I had cared for who had thiourea for treatment. Within a few weeks after getting back to Ann Arbor, I was encouraged to present this work in our Department of Internal Medicine journal club. During the war, the journal club was held in the faculty's homes in the evening because we were so busy during the day due to massive understaffing caused by the war effort.

Cyrus E. Sturgis, who was the chairman of the Department of Medicine, complimented me on my paper on antithyroid drug treatment of thyrotoxicosis.

Antithyroid Drugs Give Research Grant

Gifford Upjohn, who had been a resident of Dr. Sturgis's in the Department of Internal Medicine at University Hospital, was now the president of the Upjohn Pharmaceutical Corporation. He told Dr. Sturgis that he had a new drug to slow down the thyroid called thiouracil. Unfortunately, it was thought that thiouracil might also occasionally depress the bone marrow and kill the patient. Although Dr. Sturgis was a hematologist and therefore uniquely qualified to handle such a toxic drug reaction Dr. Upjohn wondered if Dr. Sturgis still had an interest in thyroid disease that had been promoted when he was head of thyroid disease for a relatively brief period at Peter Bent Brigham when he was in Boston (at Harvard). Dr. Sturgis said yes, he was interested and he had a man named Bill Beierwaltes in his residency program in internal medicine who may have had as much experience in this area while he was in Cleveland as anyone in the United States at that time. He explained to Gifford, however, that he wanted Gifford to give me a grant of $5,000 so that I could hire a technologist to do blood counts and all laboratory work necessary on this project because I was a good clinician and he wanted me to develop primarily as a clinician to help him take care of patients during the severe shortage of doctors during the war. Gifford agreed gladly to these considerations and so I had my first grant for research during the first year of assistant residency in 1944 at the University Hospital.

Pulmonary Tuberculosis and Artificial Pneumothorax for Five Years

This grant was very important because I had gone to bed with tuberculosis two months after being married on January 1, 1942, a little more than halfway through my internship. Since there was no treatment for tuberculosis in the form of pills available at that time, I was asked to not sit up in bed for 365 days after being put to bed. At the end of six months, my minimal tuberculosis on the left lung had done a good job of healing, but there was no regression of the minimal tuberculous lesion in my right lung. I was therefore started on an artificial pneumothorax. For five years, once a week, I had to have my lungs fluoroscoped to decide whether I was ready to have the next injection of air through a needle in the space created between the lungs and the chest wall. I also had a little fluid in the space between the lung and the chest wall, and a debate was always carried on in my presence as to whether or not I could stay out of the hospital another week to work. I thus entered into roughly five and a half years of "acute anxiety" before my lungs were declared totally healed and the pneumothorax was discontinued. This stress plus my poverty wages obviously constituted a large burden on my wife and the business of finding an apartment and then a house and starting to raise children.

However, my academic opportunities developed rapidly and outstandingly in the field of thyroid disease because of this beginning. As a 4F, exempt from military service, I could easily have had a residency at almost any good hospital in the United States. The University of Michigan Hospital won the competition because they gave me rest hours in a hospital bed on the tuberculosis floor after lunch until three o'clock in the afternoon and then two o'clock in the afternoon. I also was exempted from night calls and weekend calls. No other hospital was so thoughtful about my tuberculosis healing. John Barnwell, head of tuberculosis, deserves all the credit for that.

American Thyroid Association

Dr. Sturgis introduced me to the American Thyroid Association and James Howard Means, M.D., chairman of the Department of Medicine at Massachusetts General Hospital (Harvard) and the author of the first outstanding book on the thyroid in the United States, *Thyroid and Its Diseases* (Philadelphia: J.B. Lippincott, 1937). Richard Lyons, M.D., associate professor of internal medicine at the University of Michigan (later chairman of his own department at New York State University, Syracuse) deserves *the* credit for telling me how great my first journal club was at the University of Michigan on my internship experience with antithyroid drugs. He urged me to submit an abstract on this work to the American Thyroid Association and attend the meeting of the American Federation for Clinical Research (and Central Society for Clinical Research) each fall at the Drake Hotel in Chicago, and the Atlantic City meeting in April (American Federation for Clinical Research plus the American Society for Clinical Investigation and the Association of American Physicians).

James Howard Means, M.D., treated me just as he would if I had been one of his own Internal Medicine Thyroid Fellows at Massachusetts General Hospital. He was a wonderful role model for me.

71

My First American Thyroid Association Presentation

My first paper presented at the American Thyroid Association was "The Definitive Treatment of Thyrotoxicosis with Antithyroid Drugs" (1946). Here I defined the clinical characteristics of patients who would stay well and which patients would not stay well after stopping their drug treatment for thyrotoxicosis.

The use of antithyroid drugs also got me into the use of antithyroid drugs to treat the pregnant thyrotoxic woman. This also got me deeply into the subject of the unborn child with an underactive thyroid that results in subnormal brain and skeletal development or the reverse problem of too much thyroid hormone for the fetus that might cause premature closing of the bones of the skull (with a subnormal brain size development) and result in "cranial stenosis" or congestive heart failure and death of the child.

Goiter and Second Grant

It also got me heavily into the problem of the presence of goiters in the state of Michigan. The farmers in Wisconsin and Michigan complained massively from 1916 to 1920 to their state farm agents that they were losing large sums of money because their sheep and pigs were born hairless with "pink disease." Marine and Lenhart at Johns Hopkins University had shown in 1910 that when brook trout were maintained without iodine, their thyroid gland invariably enlarged to produce a "goiter." However, the addition of a small amount of iodine to the water caused the goiters to decrease in size.

Marine and Lenhart were hired by the states of Michigan, Wisconsin, and Ohio to investigate the cause of the pink disease in cattle because Hart had described this malady in newborn pigs and Kalkus the weakness and big neck in newborn lambs and colts. The reason the sheep and pigs were pink at birth was that iodine deficiency had led to hypothyroidism in the mother and the fetus so that the farm animals were "premature" in growth at birth and thus did not have their normal complement of white hair. Because they were "premature," they had a high neonatal death rate. Salt licks containing large amounts of iodide were then introduced into the farmyards, and the iodine deficiency and hypothyroidism were relieved in farm animals.

In 1952, Brock Brush, Chairman of the Iodized Salt Committee of the Michigan State Medical Society, and J. K. Altland of the Michigan Department of Health, remarked, "It is difficult to believe, but it is true, that animals have received better therapy than the people in many goiter areas."

The cows' milk then produced high quantities of iodide, which then decreased the incidence of iodine-deficient goiters in humans and prevented hypothyroidism in the pregnant mother and her fetus. The use of iodized salt for humans was instituted but not required. The law stated that wherever salt was sold, iodized salt must also be sold. Thus, the beneficial effect in humans was primarily from treatment of sheep and cattle.

In addition to the farmers' concerns about their livestock, the draft board findings during World War I generated interest in "endemic goiter" in humans. In the 1919 edition of *The Journal of the Michigan State Medical Society*, Levin reported that, "Goiter was so prevalent in some groups, that as high as 30% of 538 applicants were incapacitated for Army services, owing to disqualifying goiters." It was the incidence of goiter among recruits that led to the clinical studies on humans in Michigan.[1]

It was then decided that dairy herds should also eat out of special stainless steel troughs and that these should be cleaned with an antiseptic called Betadine. This was loaded with milligrams of iodide, and the cows produced milk with even higher iodine content. It was also found that cows developed fungus infection on their hooves, and so these were treated with Betadine and the cows thus ingested even more iodide and produced more iodine in the milk. Then, farmers were sold iodide kits for iodinating their drinking water because it was cheaper and easier than putting chlorine in the drinking water in their wells. Thus, even more iodide was ingested by humans.

1. W. H. Beierwaltes, "The most common thyroid disease in the state of Michigan is endemic goiter due to iodine deficiency," *Washtenaw County Medical Society Newsletter* 39 (September 1987): 3–10.

This increased iodine ingestion produced a disease in humans called Hashimoto's struma, which led to hypothyroidism and goiter. I demonstrated this disease in dogs and produced it in dogs and published on these mechanisms and produced the explanation in the *Bulletin of the All-India Institute of Medical Sciences* in India (July/October 1969).

Because of a high persistence of goiter after all this in the state of Michigan and because of people in their twenties to forties who had IQs of 40 due to untreated hypothyroidism at birth, I was able to obtain a grant of $40,000 from the state of Michigan to study this problem within the state of Michigan. We reviewed all of the "cretins" at the University Hospital and all of the cretins in the state mental institutions in the state of Michigan. One of our articles that excited a great deal of interest then and up to the present was "Congenital Hypothyroidism, a Preventable Cause of Mental Retardation."

Radio-iodine for Diagnosis and Treatment of Disease: Nuclear Medicine, a New Medical Specialty

First Course for Physicians

Dr. Sturgis heard and read that the new United States Atomic Energy Commission in Oak Ridge, Tennessee, was going to release to qualified individuals radioactive isotopes including radioactive iodine for the study of thyroid gland metabolism. He told me that, of course, I would want to do this. He told me that there would be a course at Oak Ridge for interested doctors on a first-come, first-served basis, and he made certain that I got off to this course. Thus, I was one of the first doctors in the United States to have some training in this area.

First Textbook for Physicians

As soon as I returned, the other doctors at the University Hospital wanted to learn everything that I had learned in Oak Ridge. One of my residents, Phil Johnson, and I started to teach the doctors. Phil suggested we write a book on this subject instead of constantly making copies of our lectures. We did and titled it, *The Clinical Use of Radioisotopes* by Beierwaltes, Johnson and Solari (W. B. Saunders Co., Philadelphia, 1958). It was the second best-seller of that corporation for many years (the number one best-seller was *Conn's Current Therapy*). Countless later acquaintances told me that this book precipitated their decision to enter the new specialty of "nuclear medicine."

New Method of Treating Cancer

In this new book, I laid out my approach to the treatment of thyroid cancer that became *the* method in 95 percent of hospitals in the United States and 85 percent of hospitals outside the United States. This statement was made in 1983 at the presentation of the largest monetary research prize I have ever received, Johann-Georg-Zimmerman Trust for Cancer Research, science prize for 1982–83, German Radiology Congress, Hannover, Germany.

We were the first to insist on a total surgical thyroidectomy as the first step in treating all patients with thyroid cancer. The second step was to keep the patient off thyroid hormone for six weeks. The third step was to do a radio-iodine scan of the neck and whole body to look for thyroid remnant or thyroid cancer remnant or metastasis. We then gradually found that the usually effective dose of radio-iodine for treatment was (1) 150 millicuries to ablate the thyroid remnant; (2) 175 millicuries for regional node metastasis; and (3) 200 millicuries for spreads outside the neck. The next step was to put the patient on thyroid hormone for one year. After that one year, the thyroid hormone was discontinued for six weeks (to allow us to scan the patient's entire body for cancer spread remnant), after which time it was restarted for another year. The last step was to check the patient one year later. If any cancer was found, a dose of two hundred millicuries of radio-iodine was given and the patient was put back on thyroid hormone to be rechecked again after one year. If the patient was then free of his/her disease by all criteria, the patient was to have a recheck with a total body scan every five years, off thyroid hormone for six weeks, until he or she was lost to follow-up.

Dr. Sturgis thought it was time for us to have a radioactive isotope unit for clinical studies in the hospital and got the head of the surgery department, Fred Coller, and the head of the radiology department, Fred Hodges, to agree to making me chief of this unit in 1952. Thus, Dr. Furstenberg, the dean of the medical school, and Kerlikowski, the director of the hospital, with these agreements, gave me a five-room suite on the third floor of the old hospital for a nuclear medicine division. The national "Society of Nuclear Medicine" was started, and several of us, including John Lawrence of Berkeley,[1] worked long and hard to create the separate specialty of nuclear medicine.

In the meantime, workers at both Harvard and UCLA used radioactive iodine to concentrate in the human thyroid gland and through the irradiation with beta rays to slow down the thyroid and cure the overactivity of the thyroid with one dose. Seidlen and Marinelli at New York State University first tried to treat a thyroid cancer with radioactive iodine. I was so terribly impressed with this dramatic and important development in the treatment of overactive thyroid and thyroid cancer that I decided to devote the rest of my academic career to the development of other drugs that would take radioactive iodine into other cancers for diagnosis and treatment.

First Radio-iodine-Labeled Antibodies for Diagnosis and Treatment of Cancer

The average radiation therapist would give his right arm to get 5,000 rads of radiation into any cancer. Thyroid tissue possesses the unique property of concentrating iodine up to two hundred times greater in thyroid cells than other cells in the body. In addition, in 85 percent of disintegrations of radioactive iodine, intensely ionizing beta rays are released that only go up to 3 mm in tissue. Thus, the radioactive iodine only goes where it is needed and only irradiates the tissue that one is trying to slow down or get rid of. Thus, we can deliver up to 100,000 rads of radiation per 100 millicuries of radioactive iodine. The only limitation is that, when you get up to a 250-rad blood dose, you might start depressing the bone marrow. This is prevented by giving the patient a tracer dose of radioactive iodine and quantitating the blood and urine concentrations for a *minimum* of twenty-four hours before deciding the safe dose and giving the treatment dose.

---

1. John Lawrence's brother, Ernest Lawrence, received a Nobel Prize for inventing the cyclotron.

It occurred to me that this new treatment of cancer was superior to all previous methods of treating cancer because (1) the patient merely swallowed some water (which contained the treatment dose of I^{131}) through a straw and did not taste or feel anything; (2) the patient did not vomit from treatment as with chemotherapy; (3) the patient did not lose his hair from the irradiation as with chemotherapy; (4) the patient left the hospital after a two- to three-day stay to function normally; (5) the cancer may disappear completely and permanently in as short a time as three months after the treatment dose; and (6) the patient may not need more than the one dose.

I therefore committed myself to continuing the radio-iodine treatment of thyroid cancer and also to developing new pharmaceuticals designed to be labeled with radioactive iodine to target diagnostically and therapeutically in cancers other than thyroid (which is the only one treatable with just one dose of solution by mouth).

Even today, when we have CAT scanning, nuclear magnetic resonance, and ultrasound, these new radiologic imaging techniques only show when a tumor or a cancer or spread of the cancer to lymph nodes is present and how big it is. Since radioactive iodine is the only thing that cures thyroid cancer, only a radioactive iodine tracer dose and total body scan tell you whether you have a treatable or curable thyroid cancer.

In 1950, one of my technicians, Charlie Knorpp, came out of the war to work for me in the clinical radioisotope unit. He wanted to get a master's degree furnished by the United States government. I suggested that he get a master's degree in immunology with the head of immunology, Charles Nungester. Charles was delighted and asked me what project I suggested. I suggested that we label antibodies against cancer with radioactive iodine. This eventually led to me treating a patient with a rapidly progressive malignant melanoma with seven metastases to the lungs and forty-five metastases to the skin of his abdomen after surgical resection of the original primary in the right groin and present in numerous lymph nodes. I gave this patient the treatment dose on December 10, 1951, using a continuous intravenous drip of radiolabeled antibody solution against the melanoma whole cancer cells.

To make a long story short, I became acknowledged as being the first person in the world to treat a cancer patient with radioiodine-labeled antibodies. That patient had a total disappearance of all of his cancer and, when he was killed in an automobile accident nine years later, an autopsy disclosed that he was indeed free of his malignant melanoma. Although we tried to reproduce this experiment and failed, the dramatic colored pictures that I took at that time thrill everybody with inspiration to repeat this work.

In 1971, I first succeeded in producing "radioimmunodiagnosis" with radiolabeled antibodies in a human cancer transplanted to under the skin in the golden hamster.

In the spring of 1993, Richard Kern, president of the Cytogen Corporation, called me and said that he had a "win-win" proposition for me. He said that I had been the first person in the world to ever treat a cancer with radioiodine-labeled antibodies in 1951 and the first person in the world to ever produce radioimmunodiagnosis in 1972, while he, with his Cytogen Corporation, had finally succeeded in getting the first radio-iodine-labeled antibody approved for routine clinical use by the Food and Drug Administration process of years and now had a radiolabeled antibody that could do radioimmunodiagnosis localization for cancer of the ovary, colon, and breast. He therefore proposed that we present this to the media in the nuclear medicine division at the University of Michigan to give proper academic notoriety for his corporation for doctors to start using it routinely. This was done on January 22, 1993.

In September of 1994, Richard Wahl, whom I had recruited in 1983 to start taking over my work in this field, published a paper in *The New England Journal of Medicine* on work carried out at the University of Michigan with several other authors, including Dr. Kaminsky as the senior author (8/12/93). They had treated twenty patients with the most rapidly developing and most fatal cancer today consisting of non-Hodgkin's lymphoma with radio-iodinated antibodies. These patients had failed to respond to all other forms of treatment. The tumors shrank in 50 percent of the patients and completely disappeared in 50 percent.

79

This led to the company that produced the antigen and antibody receiving three thousand telephone calls the first day after the publication of this article in *The New England Journal of Medicine* and two thousand telephone calls a day for the next two days and then one thousand telephone calls a day. That same day, August 12, the *Ann Arbor News* published a one-third-page interview they had with the senior author, Dr. Kaminsky. They asked him how long he had devoted to this important breakthrough in cancer treatment. He said that he had worked on it for two years. On September 2, the *Ann Arbor News* published a one-third-page article by Richard Wahl with the headline that William H. Beierwaltes, M.D. had published the first treatment of a cancer in a human (malignant metastatic melanoma) forty years previously (1951) and the first "radioimmunodiagnosis" in 1971. It was also pointed out that I had recruited Dr. Wahl to join me in this effort in 1983. By that time I was already using monoclonal antibodies (for which Kohler and Milstein received a Nobel Prize) labeled with radioactive iodine in humans with cancer for attempted radioimmunodiagnosis and treatment. See Appendix 1 (letter from Peter Ward).

Radiopharmaceuticals to Image Tumors of the Adrenal Cortex, the Adrenal Medulla, and Malignant Melanoma

As we began to get good grants from the National Institutes of Health and the Atomic Energy Commission in the early 1960s, my colleague, Ed Carr, and I decided to bring in topnotch medicinal and organic chemists as well as physicists to help us in these successful efforts. We first brought in Ray Counsell from the Abbott Corporation on a research grant from the American Cancer Society.[2]

---

2. I was a member of the American Cancer Society Research Personnel Committee from 1960 until 1967.

Since the secretions from the adrenal cortex (steroids) contain a high concentration of cholesterol, we showed first that the carbon-14-labeled cholesterol did concentrate in the adrenal cortex in animals (1970). Ray then made a radio-iodinated cholesterol (19-iodocholesterol), and this succeeded in producing diagnostic localization and differential diagnosis in a wide variety of tumors of the adrenal cortex (1971). We received high praise for the work in *The New England Journal of Medicine* editorial and in the *Yearbook of Nuclear Medicine* (1971).

In experiments on developing drugs to treat malignant melanomas, I used carbon-14-labeled precursors of the final melanin pigment (1969).

Whenever we sacrificed the rats or hamsters to determine the radioactivity concentration in a wide variety of tissues and organs, there was a strikingly high concentration of the radio-labeled compound only in the adrenal gland. We then proved that this was in the adrenal medulla (the inside of the adrenal gland). It occurred to me that there was a common pathway of uptake of the melanin precursors and the adrenaline precursors.

Counsell began work on radio-labeled imaging agents from the adrenal medulla. I brought in an organic chemist, Don Wieland. We were first successful in imaging the adrenal medulla with radio-labeled enzyme inhibitors in November 1976 and with I^{131} iodobenzy guanidine in 1979. These compounds were in such demand that we acquired patents on them and started two international manufacturing "corporations" for "Orphan Drugs" for the F.D.A. Much to my amusement, I found that the F.D.A. referred to me on paper as president of a radio-pharmaceutical corporation. This work was done in the reactor building on the north campus with the permission of Bill Kerr, Ph.D., Head of the Department of Nuclear Engineering, and, of course, all under the control of the University of Michigan.

We also developed some radio-iodinated precursors of melanin that we used to treat malignant melanomas with clear-cut benefit in the golden hamster and in one human with a big recurrent malignant melanotic melanoma on the anterior thigh of the left leg (1970).

81

The First Chromosomal Explanation
of the Origin of Thyroid Cancer

I visited the National Cancer Institute as a guest of Jacob Robbins to choose a rat thyroid gland cancer that most closely simulated the most common thyroid cancer in humans. I looked at the microscope slides and selected the tumor I wanted and then had Jacob teach me how to feed these rats an iodine-deficient diet. The iodine-deficient diet makes the thyroid gland less efficient in producing thyroid hormone. The pituitary gland makes the thyroid gland work harder to produce adequate quantities of thyroid hormone. We showed, using a new technique of picturing all the chromosomes in the nuclei of the cells (karyotyping) that, when the thyroid works harder, the thyroid cells are enlarged and increase their rate of cell division. The nuclei start making mistakes in cell division. At first there is an increased number of chromosomes in each cell nucleus above normal ("hyperploidy"), then less than normal, then dropping out of the #15 chromosome, then the appearance of huge bizarre chromosomes.

Goiters of rats, transplanted subcutaneously, became non-palpable, then grew with one of three characteristic chromosomal patterns, suggested that these transplanted neoplasms grow from a single cell or a clone of cells in the parent goiter. The characteristics of these TSH (thyroid-stimulating hormone)-dependent, transitional and autonomous tumors are shown (see table 58.1, page 1320, *Werner's the Thyroid*, fifth edition). The table shows that the TSH-dependent tumors disappeared and were not palpable within five months in the control hosts. The transitional tumors and autonomous tumors did become palpable within five months. Their growth rate was increased by iodine deficiency in the dependent and transitional tumors but not in the autonomous tumors. The growth rate of the dependent tumor was 3.31 grams per month, of the transitional tumor 6.2 grams per month, and of the autonomous tumor 41.8 grams per month. The pathology type was adeno- and follicular carcinomas in the dependent, follicular and papillary carcinomas in the transitional, and anaplastic carcinoma in the autonomous.

With continued TSH stimulation, the thyroid tissue was required to work harder and speed up the rate of cell division. The nuclei, being pushed to go faster, began to make mistakes (like a technician doing his or her work in the laboratory) and there began to be both hyperploidy and hypoploidy (increased numbers of chromosomes and decreased numbers of chromosomes above the modal number of forty-two chromosomes). The dependent tumors had 82 percent of the cells retaining the modal number of forty-two chromosomes. The transitional tumors had 42.8 percent and the autonomous had 40 percent. The dependent tumors retained both chromosomes of pair #15, but in 3.8 percent of the cells, one was missing. In the transitional tumors, 39 percent were missing a modal number and in autonomous tumors, 64 percent were missing a modal number.

Finally, the next change was that large macrochromosomes began to appear in the nuclei of the cells. These large macrochromosomes were only found in 1.9 percent of the cells in the dependent tumor, in 4.8 percent of the cells in the transitional tumor, and in 70 percent of the cells in the autonomous tumor. The process of developing "anaplastic" carcinoma is that the cells thus so disturbed begin to look less and less like thyroid cells and they spread (metastasize) widely all over the body and kill the host animal (in this case, laboratory rats) within a few weeks. The technicians actually became afraid that they might get some of those cells in themselves, even though they knew that rat cells can't grow in a human. Further details of this work and its relationship to the natural history of human thyroid cancer are given in my article on the natural history of thyroid cancer in chapter 58 of *Werner's the Thyroid, fifth edition* (edited by Ingbar and Braverman) on pages 1319 to 1329. This pioneering work on the chromosomal origin of thyroid cancer in rats was confirmed in humans and every detail was published and related in other articles to our forty-year experience in treating thyroid cancer with radioactive iodine in the human. This work also attracted the attention of the British Imperial Cancer Foundation, and I was invited to present this work there. The famous British thyroid surgeon, Selwyn Taylor, dean of the Royal Post-Graduate Medical School, was my host.

X-Ray Treatment of Thyroid Eye Disease
("Barbara Bush Disease")

Our first three articles on the development of X-ray therapy behind the eyeball in the treatment of progressive protrusion of the eyes associated with thyroid gland overactivity assumed considerable interest when Ken Burman, the thyroid physician for Barbara Bush when she developed progressive protrusion of her eyes, using this technique successfully in helping to improve her condition.

The Excitement of Research—
Hereditary Increase in TBG

I will spend some time on one topic because of the exciting way this whole problem and its solution developed. This was my research on the familial and hereditary increase in the thyroxin binding sites in the serum alpha globulin that resulted in an increased concentration of thyroid hormone in the blood.

In 1958, an outstanding professor of renal physiology at the University of Michigan called me to ask for my consultation and help. He said that he had gone to a PTA meeting at the University High School and a pediatrician lectured to the parents there telling them that children who had congenital hypothyroidism could have decreased IQs as a result of the lack of thyroid hormone for the child's brain development. He thought that it was always possible that acquisition of underactivity of the thyroid gland after birth could produce reading difficulties without overt hypothyroidism. He therefore wanted to study this by getting blood thyroid functions tests on not only the children in school who were having reading difficulties but also the parents of those children.

My colleague Walter and his wife submitted to these tests. The principal test used was the serum protein-bound iodine, which measures iodine in the 4-iodine molecule of the 4-iodine atom thyroid hormone and also the 3-iodine atom hormone. Walter's serum protein-bound iodine was considerably above normal. The pediatrician therefore called Walter and told him that he was sick from thyrotoxicosis. He suggested that Walter call me for confirmation of the diagnosis and treatment because I had founded the thyroid clinic at the University of Michigan in 1944 and was chief of the clinical unit and also the thyroid research laboratory at the hospital.

I asked Walter if he felt sick. He said no, he felt fine. I knew that iodine contrast material for X-ray examinations such as a cholecystogram to look at the gallbladder, etc., would cause spurious elevation of the serum protein-bound iodine. He told me that he had never had any such test or intravenous injection. I also told him that, if he had been taking female sex hormone in any form, this would also have spuriously elevated the serum protein-bound iodine because female sex hormone increases the rate of synthesis of a serum protein, thyroxin-binding globulin. He denied all such possibilities.

I therefore said, "Walter, if you don't have any spurious cause for an elevated serum protein-bound iodine, then you have a disease that has not yet been described." Little did I know that this would turn out to be true and that I would describe it.

We had just published an article for the first time standardizing serum protein quantitation with a popular Spinco-Durram electrophoresis apparatus. Jack Robbins had just published in the *Journal of Clinical Investigation* in 1958 a new method of reverse-flow electrophoresis for quantitating thyroxin in human serum. He had just shown these changes in the serum protein-bound iodine and thyroxin-binding capacity in pregnancy and the decrease after methyltestosterone. When Walter called me on March 17, 1958, his complete history and physical examination showed no abnormality to suggest thyroid or other endocrine problem. His two sons, ages eighteen and twelve, and his daughter, age fifteen, also presented no abnormal findings by medical history or physical examination except for the history of allergic asthma treated with potassium iodine in his twelve-year-old son. Walter was found to have serum protein-bound iodine and butanol-extractable iodine (BEI) levels ranging between two and three times normal and maintained over an observation period of nine months.

We had also developed the radio-iodine-labeled tri-iodothyronine erythrocyte uptake test, and this had suggested that the serum protein-bound iodine elevation was related to increased affinity of the plasma proteins for thyroid hormone. Robbins and Rall had also just published the thyroxin-binding capacity of serum in normal man in the excellent *Journal of Clinical Investigation* in 1955. No abnormality was detected in thyroxine binding to albumin or prealbumin. We showed that, although the extrathyroidal organic iodine pool was expanded to roughly the same size as that found in patients with untreated thyrotoxicosis, the degradation rate in micrograms of thyroxine per day was within the normal range. As a result, such affected persons had no change in their health. However, a doctor, finding an increase in the amount of thyroid hormone in the blood, might misdiagnose and treat the patient for an overactive thyroid gland.

At this point, Walter asked the question, if this abnormality in his blood proteins was presumably congenital, could it have been inherited? I was delighted to have him lead me down this path and said, yes, we would like to study his children if he was in agreement. He thought it was a good idea. His daughter but not his two sons also had elevated serum protein-bound iodine and BEI levels and a subnormal 131-I T3 RBC uptake and an elevated thyroxin-binding protein capacity, constituting evidence that the abnormality was familial and could conceivably be hereditary. This finding, for the first time showing such markedly increased levels of thyroid hormone in the serum of euthyroid individuals (i.e., those with normal thyroid function), supported the contention that the total serum thyroid hormone concentration did not alone govern the metabolic status of the individual.

I told Walter that we should study his family to see whether this abnormality was inherited and what the mechanism of inheritance was. Walter said that this would be impossible because all of his family lived in one small town in England. A few minutes later, I opened my mail and found that the American Thyroid Association was going to have its every-five-years international meeting in London in June and that Jock and Jay Whitney at the American embassy had offered to our colleagues in Washington, D.C. the opportunity for members of the American Thyroid Association to get into the Fourth of July celebration at the American embassy in London on a first-come, first-served basis. Since the number of opportunities was limited, they suggested that we send in the form immediately requesting this audience. I did so and then told Walter that I would like to study his family. He told me that he would be glad to write them but reminded me that I would have to find a laboratory at the local hospital where his family lived to draw the blood specimens, centrifuge them, and prepare them for being sent back to our laboratory in the United States for study.

I left my laboratory in the Kresge Building somewhat depressed about this problem and ran into a professor of gastroenterology in our department who introduced me to a friend with whom he was walking. The friend turned out to be a professor of gastroenterology in the town where Walter's relatives lived. I told him the problem and found out that he was just as interested in sailing as I was. He said that he would be delighted to furnish the laboratory and help in drawing the bloods and centrifuging the specimens.

I told Walter and he wrote his relatives. He doubted that a letter from me or from him would motivate his relatives in full numbers to be there for the blood drawing. Ultimately, one of his relatives was intensely interested in human genetics and was fascinated by this project. (The principal motivation we furnished them was that they might have the blood drawn by a doctor who didn't know that this abnormality of the serum proteins existed without any disease caused by it. It would then cost them a lot of money and they might end up with the wrong diagnosis and treatment.) "The geneticist" got on the telephone and called each relative and told them that if they had any trouble getting there, he would personally pick them up, but he wanted to make certain that they would be there for the blood drawing. I am convinced, in retrospect, that without his help we could not have completed a thorough study of the family.

In the meantime, I had been contacted by an Australian internal medicine resident who was currently in the research laboratory of Roitt and Doniach in London. They had been teaching him for one year intensively in immunology, particularly as it pertained to Hashimoto's struma, which caused hypothyroidism. They had told him that he should now go to a good clinical thyroidology division in the United States that had a good laboratory, and because of our recent publications, they suggested he contact me. At the same time, I got an acceptance for my wife, Mary-Martha, and me to come to the Fourth of July celebration at the American Embassy in London. I told Ian, this internal medicine resident, that I would contact him to have an interview with him at that time.

When the day arrived and we were standing in the long waiting line in the beautiful gardens of the American embassy to meet Jock and Jay Whitney, I engaged the naval officer immediately behind me in conversation. It turned out that he was Commander Fugit of the United States Navy in the American Embassy office. I asked him what he could do. He said that he could facilitate the exchange of blood across the Atlantic that might be difficult through normal channels. I told him that I had just been told that it would be impossible to send blood specimens across the Atlantic from London because of government restrictions. He said it would be impossible unless I could have a doctor in a nearby hospital immediately available to bring the bloods to him on practically a moment's notice when he found that he had an appropriate shipment to include these specimens in to be sent to the United States.

My interview with Ian went off beautifully and he was, of course, accepted in my laboratory for further training. He told me where I could bring the bloods as soon as they were drawn and that he would keep them instantly ready while waiting to hear from Commander Fugit. I therefore notified Commander Fugit of these wonderful serendipitous events that had happened and gave him the telephone number.

We had as close to a 100 percent turnout of Walter's relatives as one could have and had a wonderful time with all the people above described who were participating in this movement.

My chief research technologist, Norma Spafford, received all the bloods while we were still presenting our paper at the international meeting in London, visiting relatives in Germany, and then attending an international meeting of the Endocrine Society in Copenhagen. As soon as I got home, I submitted all of the subjects' relationships with each other and their blood values to a good geneticist in our department of genetics at the University of Michigan. The defect was inherited in the same distribution as the serum uric acid level in gout. "The Familial Increase in the Thyroxin-Binding Sites in Serum Alpha Globulin" was published in the *Journal of Clinical Investigation* in October 1959.

Every spring we had a big research meeting in Atlantic City at the biggest hall on the Boardwalk. Initially, this had been one society, the Association of American Physicians.

When these people became too old and too august, the American Society for Clinical Investigation was started. When they became too old and too august, the American Federation for Clinical Research was started by Henry Christian. The American Federation for Clinical Research soon had the largest membership of the youngest medical researchers, the American Society for Clinical Investigation second, and the Association of American Physicians was limited to roughly 250 people in the world. It was obviously the place that we would most like to present a paper. I therefore submitted an abstract to the Association of American Physicians on the hereditary increase in the thyroxin-binding sites in the serum alpha globulin. I was deliriously happy when it was accepted for presentation. I then devoted an extraordinary amount of time preparing for that presentation, particularly to make sure that the slides were perfect. I had risen in the ranks of the American Federation for Clinical Research to become its national president 1954–55. Most people did not become a member of the Association of American Physicians unless they had described a new disease, diagnosis of a disease, or a new treatment of a disease. Perhaps because I had described a new diagnosis and disease, I became a member of the Association of American Physicians in 1966.

Almost immediately and almost automatically, I was contacted by Marquis *Who's Who in America* and also Marquis *World Who's Who in Science*, "From Antiquity to the Present." Needless to say, I was immediately given a Guggenheim Fellowship Award in 1966–67 and a Commonwealth Fund Award in 1967 to take a sabbatical.

I had already been promoted to full professor on July 1,

1959, but I did have much more success in getting invitations to go to other universities all over the world to lecture and getting written offers to go elsewhere, thus successfully encouraging the University of Michigan to increase my salary. Each of these steps also increased my ability to get new grants and laboratory space. When I told my friends that I hated to accept all these invitations to lecture elsewhere and leave my wife home alone, they suggested that I tell my inviters that I couldn't go without their paying her way as well as mine. This turned out to be no problem, and so Mary-Martha and I did not have to postpone travel together until after I retired. A friend estimated that one of our sources of happiness in the poverty of academic salaries was about a $20,000-a-year travel budget for Mary-Martha and me not paid by the University of Michigan or by my research grants.

During this same period of time, I was moving up in offices in the American Thyroid Association from program chairman to vice president. We sponsored a meeting of the American Thyroid Association in Ann Arbor. The European Society of Nuclear Medicine for many years invited me to lecture in a different country in Europe (with Mary-Martha) in association with a different country in Europe sponsoring their annual meeting. Unfortunately, this meeting occurred at exactly the same time as the American Thyroid Association meeting. An embarrassment here was avoided by the fact that Bob Kroc's brother, who had founded the most famous hamburger company in the world, McDonald's, suddenly announced to the officers of the American Thyroid Association that his brother had set up a huge foundation for medical research and asked Bob to choose whom he wished to receive this money. For some reason or other, the American Thyroid Association suddenly decided that Bob would become president immediately. Later, the officers of the American Thyroid Association felt very badly about this omission of a presidency after sponsoring a meeting and gave me a distinguished service award in 1973, which was awarded to me in my absence while I attended the European Society of Nuclear Medicine meeting in another country.

In retrospect, it is also of interest that I was simultaneously moving up the officer hierarchy in the Society of Nuclear Medicine. I had become a member in 1958, the treasurer in 1960, chairman of the membership committee in 1963–64, president-elect in 1964–65, and president in 1965–66 simultaneously with my becoming a member of the Association of American Physicians.

Success—the Ultimate Stress

Along with the acquisition of increased research grants and increased research laboratory space and a wide variety of Ph.D.s in physics, chemistry, and immunology, we were also asked to design a new clinical nuclear-medicine division to be put in the new proposed University Hospital. Considerable evidence was produced that, whether or not your medical school made the top ten was based not only on increased funding from grants because of recognition in the peer-review process, but also on a modern university hospital facility to attract the most outstanding clinicians who were capable of getting the most outstanding grants. Funds were then provided for an update in our clinical instrumentation, such as single-photon-emission CAT scanners and a marked increase in computer facilities to handle the increased data from this newer instrumentation. Indeed when one "request for a proposal" went out to the scientific community, some of my friends accused me of having written it. This was because the proposal stated that, if you had the following personnel, the following equipment, and the following space, etc., then it would be appropriate for you to apply for that grant. They pictured me as the one they thought of first having all this equipment and space and personnel, and therefore they assumed that I had written the request for the proposal.

The PET Grant

One day I sat in the audience at a national meeting of the Society of Nuclear Medicine while David Kuhl from UCLA gave a presentation on his development of the positron emission transaxial tomograph scanner and how he was able to detect an inherited brain disease by imaging a biochemical abnormality in the brain that led to the disease. I also heard from friends that NIH was ripe for a request for a proposal on positron emission transaxial tomography for the study of brain metabolism in health and disease through their neurologic institute. The invention of the CAT scanner had already markedly decreased our number of brain scans.

When I started to recruit in nuclear magnetic resonance imaging, Bernie Agranoff, who had just been made head of the Department of Neurosciences and in Neurology, told me how interested he was in developing this in the Division of Neurosciences and in Neurology. I also learned that the University of Michigan Medical School was recruiting for a new head of Neurology. I participated in this recruitment because I knew that a very strong chairman of the Department of Neurology would be interested in and very eager to join a medical school that had a PET scanner on its list for the future. We were fortunate in obtaining Sid Gilman as head of Neurology. He had been an endowed professor of neurology at Columbia University at the age of thirty-two. We brought him successfully to the University of Michigan as chairman of the Department of Neurology. He stated that our division of nuclear medicine furnished a strong motivation because of its interest in competency in brain imaging.

When the request for the proposal came out, it soon became evident that the top universities in the United states would apply. I invited Bernie and Sid to become co-principal investigators with me. They eagerly accepted. The title of our proposal was "Positron Emission Transaxial Tomography Scanning in the Study of the Metabolism of the Human Brain in Health and Disease." After the proposal was written, using the talents and knowledge of a wide variety of people in our three divisions and departments, endless proofreading and changes had to go on. Then, of course, we had to prepare for a project site visit, which required hundreds of hours of practice and criticism of each other, our slides, etc.

During that time, I would try to get everything out of the way and get quieted down so that I could sleep on Sunday night. Sid Gilman called me one Sunday night at eleven o'clock to tell me that a "friend" of mine, who was head of radiology at a well-known university, had been present at a review of our grant proposal and had talked against it for thirty minutes in great detail. Sid, therefore, very properly proposed that we hold a series of meetings after discussion with the people who knew all the details and revise the grant. We finally got an award of the largest of these grants and the only one that paid for, not only the positron emission transaxial tomography scanner and the accompanying cyclotron to produce the short-lived radioactive isotopes called positron emitters, but also the building that was to house them. It also provided all of the chemical and physical laboratories and personnel necessary to carry out this huge operation. Thus, we were able to build a $13 million facility and were told to immediately hire the people whose salaries were listed on the grant before we had the space for them.

I soon found that everybody wanted the money on which I was the principal investigator. The vice president for finance at the university wanted money, the dean of the medical school wanted money, and many others who had money also wanted money. A graphic illustration of how great a stress all this was to all of us is exemplified by the fact that one of the key members of our committee got a divorce during the process and his son committed suicide.

Osteoarthritis of the Hip

In about 1979, I began to have pain in my left hip and immediately decided it was osteoarthritis. The pain increased in severity, especially from 1979 till 1982 in spite of the latest varieties of medication for this pain. I therefore had a total left hip replacement on November 28, 1982. For the two years prior to the surgery, I had severe pain twenty-four hours a day, seven days a week, and spent much of my spare time in bed doing office work. I have never had symptoms since the total hip replacement and have not once had to take aspirin.

As it came time for me to retire at age sixty-nine by university rulings, I got an extension through the Board of Regents to do it at age seventy. I therefore started my Emeritus status July

1, 1987. My grant support peaked at about that time and is shown below in active grants through June 30, 1986.[3]

I was encouraged to get all of these grants transferred into the hands of outstanding younger people whom I had acquired as associates and to help recruit my successor. Bill Kelly was the chairman of the Department of Internal Medicine and was an absolute superstar. With my advice, he appointed a distinguished committee of five to come to the University of Michigan for the week. He gave them a two-inch-thick handout of the history and the strengths and weaknesses of the nuclear medicine division. His effort was to find out who would be the ideal person with what strengths to replace my strengths in view of the changes that would occur after I left.

This committee told him that my Division of Nuclear Medicine was the best in the world at that time. He was able to successfully recruit Dr. David Kuhl, who was professor of radiology at UCLA and had actually built the first PET scanner himself and was a leader in that field. By the time I retired, we had three other PET scanners paid for through other sources.

3. NCI #R01 CA33802-02 "Monoclonal Antibody Detection and Therapy of Cancer," P.I.—W. H. Beierwaltes, current yr $85,472, 09/83–08/86; D.O.E. #DE-AC02763V02031, "Radiopharmaceuticals for Diagnosis and Treatment," P.I.—W. H. Beierwaltes, current yr. $118,972, 01/85–12/87; NCI #T32 CA90915-09, "Cancer Research Training in Nuclear Medicine," Program Director—W. H. Beierwaltes, current yr $123,240, 07/84–03/98; NIAMDD 2 RO1 21477-07, "Radionuclide Adrenal Imaging in Hypertension," P.I.—J. C. Sisson, $141,035, 12/84–11/87; NINCDS P01 NS15655-06 "PET Study of Biochemistry and Metabolism of the CNS," P.I.—W. H. Beierwaltes, $1,081,499, 12/84–11/89.

Charlie Christie's Model Boat Club, Saginaw Junior High School. Ages 13–15.

First sailboat, "Pram." Designed by Christie. Built by brother Jack. My father had us row 30 miles in one day from the Saginaw River in Saginaw, Michigan, to the Bay City Yacht Club (25 miles) and then across Saginaw Bay to our first cottage at Killarney Beach. Age 13.

Second sailboat, "The Flying Dutchman." Designed by Christie. Built by Jack's best friend, Fred Klein. The author and Lyman Bittman sailed it 35 miles across Saginaw Bay from our second cottage at Aplin Beach to Point Lookout to visit our friends at this resort and returned to Aplin. Age 15.

Third sailboat, "Snipe." Class by Cosby in *Rudder* magazine. Built by the author at age 15 under the tutelage and in the basement of Charlie Christie. Bob Beckley and the author sailed it 35 miles across Saginaw Bay and 18 miles of Lake Huron to Tawas Bay to race in the annual one-week-long regatta. We won the Class B Tawas Bay Yachting Association trophy and sailed back to Aplin. We competed the next year with Eric Tims as crew.

Fourth sailboat, "Sea Fever," a 14-foot Rhodes Bantam. We raced every Sunday afternoon from April through November on Barton Pond at the Barton Boat Club in Ann Arbor, Michigan. Our three children rotated as crew and skippered it on Saturday afternoons in kids' races.

Fifth sailboat, "Kit-N-Kaboodle," a 17-foot thistle by Sandy Douglas. Three of us cruised it through the North Channel in Canada and this author published, "Thistling North Channel," in *Yachting* magazine, December 1955.

John Pierpont's 42-foot Swedish ocean race, "Siskiwit." After John read my yachting article, he asked me to be his First Mate to race this in the Mackinac Races and the 1960 Newport-to-Bermuda race (starting from the west end of Lake Superior!). This was the beginning of my large boat racing and cruising career.

Sixth sailboat, "Windsong," a Columbia 36. My racing partnership raced this boat in Port-Huron-to-Mackinac races and cruised Lake Erie and Lake Huron and the North Channel in Canada.

Seventh sailboat, "Out of Reach," a Columbia 35. It replaced "Windsong" when we proved that she had a dramatic congenital defect in the
hull.

Ed Kline's Concordia yawl, "Taloa." The author was asked to be the sailing master of the boat. The picture shows the author at the helm on a spinnaker start of a Port-Huron-to-Mackinac race.

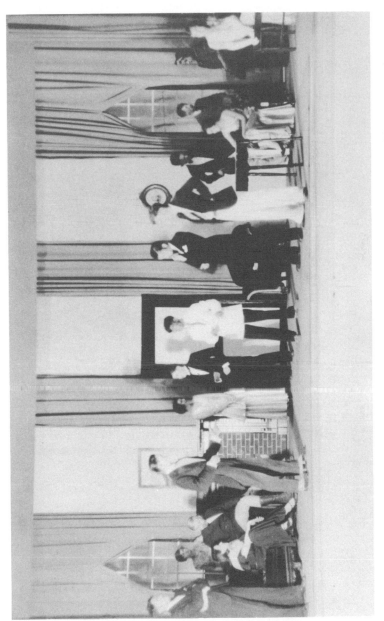

Ninth grade class play, "A Strenuous Life." The author was the leading man and is seen on the right (head in front of picture on the wall). Florence Schust, who later became one of the "17 most outstanding women in America," is seated at the small table behind me. Bonnie Milne is to the left of the door. 1930, age 14.

Carleton Mitchell in his yawl "Finesterre" near "Siskiwit" as we approached the start of the 1960 Newport-to-Bermuda race. For this racing superstar it would be his third win in a row, a feat yet to be equaled. (photo by the author)

The author in the royal Bermuda Yacht Club after the 1960 Newport-to-Bermuda race.

Larry Hagman, his wife Mai and their daughter Heidi, pose in front of our home at 1885 Fuller on May 1, 1960. They lodged in our basement apartment during his two weeks of acting in the University of Michigan Spring Drama Festival. This was well before his television fame in "I Dream of Jeannie" and as J. R. Ewing in "Dallas."

The author racing a DN iceboat on Barton Pond at speeds up to 65 miles per hour.

My beloved Mary-Martha at age 40 (a) and (b) at age 60!

The two Beierwaltes families in front of the Aplin Beach cottage. My brother Jack (at right), his sons John and William T (at left lower) and his daughter Gayle in my lap (back right). Jack's wife Ginny took the picture. William T. is now the only *great* entrepreneur in the Beierwaltes families!

Our last house in Ann Arbor, Michigan, at 1025 Forest Road in Barton Hills. The back of the house faced Barton Pond.

1942 Mary-Martha and Bill Beierwaltes 1992
Celebrating 50 years together

Our 50th wedding anniversary celebration card. Day of graduation from medical school, 1941. (Married, January 1, 1942) and summer of 1991 at Marty's cottage.

Our youngest child and only daughter, Martha Louise, with her husband, Pat, and Katie, Patrick Jr. and Colleen in front. Their big Victorian house in Petoskey, Michigan, was asked to be the site of a movie about Ernest Hemingway. Marty was referred to in the local newspaper as "The Midnight Gardener." She achieved an AB in teaching and RN and BS degrees in nursing. Pat is a cardiologist.

Our youngest son, Will, became captain of the track and football teams and was on the basketball team at University High School in Ann Arbor. Later he obtained his Ph.D. and post doctoral fellowship in hypertension at the Mayo Clinic, a senior membership on the staff of Henry Ford Hospital in Detroit, and an associate professorship of Internal Medicine at Case Western Reserved University in Cleveland. He is here with Peter, Nora and Willie.

Our oldest son Andy obtained his Bachelors in Landscape Architecture (BLA) from the University of Michigan. He was heavily in land plan systems in industry but then went into private practice as a landscape architect in Ann Arbor, Michigan. He was a walking encyclopedia long before he learned to read; why?

My First Retirement

Our House Becomes "Worthless" the Day I Retire

About the day I retired, we learned that our septic tank and disposal field for our home in Barton Hills in Ann Arbor had become worthless and there was no other place for a replacement. Thus, the consulting company told us that, in effect, our house was worthless. We had purchased it seventeen years earlier for $95,000 and were about to sell it for $400,000 when this occurred. I had just experienced a 70 percent decrease in income.

St. John Hospital and Beaumont Hospital for Seven Years

When I heard that one of my trainees, Walter DiJulio at St. John Hospital, had died of a heart attack, I asked Ed Powsner if he needed a consultant to help him get that unit going. He was delighted that I was available and interested.

When I started there, Dr. Howard Dworkin, who was head of the Department of Nuclear Medicine at William Beaumont Hospital—Royal Oak and Troy, and a former trainee of mine, was very upset because he expected me to come there. I therefore soon found myself working at Beaumont on Monday and at St. John Tuesday through Friday. I was also on night call and weekend call at age seventy for the first time in ages. When I described to my wife the commuting conditions and the salted slush on my car windshield from the expressway, she encouraged me to sell our house in Ann Arbor and purchase a house near my job at St. John Hospital.

We were delighted when she got a smaller, but very efficient

117

and comfortable house within ten minutes driving time to my office at the hospital and with no entrance on expressways. My drive was merely up East Jefferson looking at Lake St. Clair and then a left turn up Moross to the hospital. The constant sight of so many sailboats racing strongly encouraged us to buy the first sailboat of our own longer than seventeen feet. Although I was theoretically programmed to merely work there for six months and then replace myself with a younger man, we had such a good time that we were delighted to accept the suggestion of the hospital to form our own Eastside Nuclear Medicine, P.C. at St. John Hospital and I stopped working at Beaumont. I soon realized that I couldn't possibly continue to do research without laboratory space, grants, etc., which had taken forty-three years to acquire. My boss, Ed Powsner, was very supportive of all my efforts and eventually I limited myself to seeing only thyroid patients. I finally and unequivocally retired for the second time from seeing patients on August 31, 1994.

Ed Powsner urged me to continue to meet with him, Mike Joh, and the new man we had brought in to replace me, Rick Hay, M.D., Ph.D., from the University of Michigan Nuclear Medicine Division. He said that they wanted to continue to learn from me on some of their most difficult thyroid patients. I also said that I would be delighted to take up one topic each week on Tuesday after the tumor conference. While I am dictating this, I am still doing that.

Rewards of the Career

Since it is generally agreed upon that you will rarely do anything unless you are motivated, I have long ago adopted the policy of trying to find multiple motivations for any work that I can or need to do. In thinking through my daily work and career in medicine, it has been easy to identify three motivations.

Healing the Sick

Perhaps the best and perhaps genetically the strongest motivation is to provide a one-on-one direct benefit to my patients.

In taking a medical history and doing a physical examination, I have explained to patients that they are affording me a great pleasure in allowing me to be totally preoccupied without interruption for one hour and the great privilege of them honestly trying to tell me everything they know about themselves that might help me make a diagnosis and start treatment. Similarly, I consider it a great privilege for them to allow me to do a complete physical examination of their entire body to further aid me in this task. I will always remember one woman who said to me at the end of her history and physical examination, "Dr. Beierwaltes, it is probable that you know more about me than any other person in my life."

M. Scott Peck in his book, *The Road Less Traveled*, established to his satisfaction in his practice that one of the most important things that a doctor can do to help a patient's psychiatric disease is to put across to the patient by action that the doctor feels a deep sense of commitment to try to help them get well regardless of how difficult it is and how slow the progress

119

for the patient because of lying, denial, etc. Once the patient realizes *that the doctor really cares for him or her*, they are more and more willing to get well. Peck also stressed that the number one manifestation of one person caring for another, or in this case the doctor caring for the patient, is to devote all of their energy to listening to the patient. Similarly, the patient becomes more and more committed to help the doctor by taking the medication or the advice on how they can change their conduct to produce the most rapid and permanent cure.

As a result, since perhaps I am most well known internationally for curing thyroid cancer with radioactive iodine, one of the greatest thrills is to receive a letter from the mother and father of a child that I've cured of thyroid cancer metastatic to lungs. When we come to the place where I let them know that it will not be necessary for me to see their child more often than once every five years, they usually say (and not infrequently write a letter) that their child's health is the most important thing in their lives and they are well aware of the fact that, if it wasn't for me, their child would be dead from thyroid cancer.

I was brought up in the Christian religion and learned at an early age that one of the most important functions of Christ was to "heal the sick."

Teaching

A second motivation that was furnished by my academic career was to teach other students, interns, residents, technicians, nurses, and practicing physicians how to diagnose and treat their patients. Although there is not the intense relationship here that one has with his own patient, my knowledge and experience help heal a much larger number of patients than I could ever achieve in one-to-one relationships with patients.

It has been a great privilege to have so many outstanding students. For example, one of my students, Jim Wyngaarten, became head of the Department of Internal Medicine at Duke University and then head of the National Institutes of Health!

An equally high priority of Christ's was to "teach."

120

Medical Research

The third motivation in my academic career was to do research in my field in developing the specialty of nuclear medicine (the diagnosis and treatment of disease using radioactive isotopes and radioisotope-labeled pharmaceuticals). It has been rewarding to be a co-patentor of one compound to aid in the detection and localization for surgical extirpation or drug manipulation of diseases of the adrenal cortex.

Similarly, it has been rewarding to be a co-patentor of a compound to achieve this in diseases of the adrenal medulla and the tumors of the adrenal medulla. The final reward in this area was to be able to localize and directly treat the neuroblastoma, the second most common cause of death from a solid cancer in children.

And perhaps most importantly, it has been tremendously rewarding to be the first person to ever use radio-iodine-labeled antibodies for diagnosis and also for treatment of cancer. Although the clinical development of this area has taken forty years since my first treatment, it is now being used to treat the most rapidly increasing and fatal cancer there is, namely, non-Hodgkin's lymphoma. We suddenly became more aware of this disease when Jacqueline Kennedy Onassis died of it recently.

Lastly, eventually someone may be successful in finishing my early efforts to develop the radiolabeled quinolone analogs in the diagnosis and treatment of malignant melanoma and the radiolabeled enzyme inhibitors for the diagnosis and treatment of breast cancer and tumors of the adrenal cortex and adrenal medulla.

I had an owner of a ski resort in Colorado write to me that, although he had never met me personally, he wanted me to know that he had directly benefitted from my work when he went to the Mayo Clinic for diagnosis and treatment of his cancer of the adrenal medulla.

Recognition

It is most rewarding to have Tom McKearn at the Cytogen

Corporation express to me directly how grateful he is for my pioneering work in developing radiolabeled antibodies for the diagnosis and treatment of cancer. He and his team deserve great credit for getting through the Food and Drug Administration the first successful radiolabeled antibody for diagnostic localization in humans. (See appendix 1, Peter Ward's letter) Similarly, it is tremendously rewarding to me to have Richard Wahl and colleagues point out to me that I had discovered him in St. Louis when he was a diagnostic radiologist and, after he had taken several years of training in immunology, brought him into the University of Michigan to have him work with me at the stage of using monoclonal antibodies for diagnostic and therapeutic localization in cancer, and then make sure that he received 16,000 square feet of laboratory space and two of my largest grants in this area for continuing his work. Thus, when the outstanding pioneering work was published in *The New England Journal of Medicine* in September 1994, the *Ann Arbor News* and Kaminski published an article entitled, "A Major Success in Treating a Major Cancer." Richard Wahl published a large article in the *Ann Arbor News* the next day stressing in headlines that I had started this work forty years ago and continued to develop it in such a manner that it was a logical expectation for them to complete this work, this demonstration in seventeen hitherto incurable patients that the radio-iodine-labeled antibody approach to treatment of non-Hodgkin's lymphoma really worked.

It is also important to know that someone besides you feels that you have been helpful in patient care, teaching, and research. Indicators from others that you are doing well consist of promotions in rank to full professor; being chosen as a division head, being asked all over the world to be a visiting professor (with not only your way paid but your wife's way paid); receiving gold medals such as the G. V. Hevesey Lecture Medal and financial research prizes such as the Johann-George-Zimmerman Trust for Cancer Research science prize for 1982–83 from the German Radiology Congress in Hannover, Germany; having eighty-eight trainees that you have trained for two years or more give you a huge silver bowl with their names and periods that they were with me; having them establish a permanent foundation of research prizes to young residents; and particularly to have superstars like Billy Kelly as chairman of the Department of Medicine put me up in 1990 for the Distinguished Faculty Award at the University of Michigan, which was given to me in Ann Arbor on October 11, 1982. (See appendix 2)

When people brag about being in *Who's Who*, they are almost always talking about the Marquis *Who's Who in America*, which in the forty-sixth edition in 1990-91 expanded to two very large volumes. Few people seem to know that there is a much more rewarding recognition by Marquis *Who's Who*, which is a small, single volume titled *Who's Who in the World*. They have stated that this is recognition in one out of 225,000 people, that each person included in this volume is selected from out of 225,000 people who didn't make it. They have stated in their preface that the selection of a name for inclusion in *Who's Who in the World* is based on reference value.

"Some individuals become eligible for listing because of position, while others have distinguished themselves through notable achievements in their fields. Many of the listees qualify by virtue of both position and occupational attainment. In the editorial evaluation that resulted in the ultimate selection of the names in this directory, an individual's desire to be listed was not sufficient reason for inclusion; rather, it was the person's achievement that ruled. Similarly, wealth or social position was not a criterion; only occupational stature or achievement influenced selection."

Although I had been included in "The Best Doctors in America" in the 1979 first edition by the Reveil Publications initially presented in *Town and Country Magazine*, the new book by Naifeh and Smith (Woodward and White), *The Best Doctors in America in 1992*, was a great thrill because I was then engaged in full-time private practice of medicine (from 1987 to 1994). I was in both the 1992–93 and the 1993–94 editions. These doctors were selected on the basis of 17,000 telephone calls from our peers.

It was also a tremendous thrill to be selected by the American Medical Association for the highest Scientific Achievement Award of any doctor in the United States at the AMA headquarters in June 1994. The inscription on the award reads:

William H. Beierwaltes, M.D.

Clinician, teacher, investigator, Dr. William Beierwaltes has had a distinguished career in nuclear medicine and thyroidology.

As a clinician, he is perhaps best known for his early espousal of the now established treatment for thyroid cancer, combining surgical and radio-iodine therapy in a manner calculated to minimize late recurrences.

As a teacher, he organized one of the first university programs for training in nuclear medicine. His trainees are now directors of nuclear medicine throughout the world.

As an investigator, his contributions include (1) the successful use of radioimmunotherapy for non-Hodgkin's lymphoma, (2) the first successful detection of cancer with radiolabeled antibodies, which is now a routine nuclear medicine technique, (3) development of the thesis that lymphocytic thyroiditis (Hashimoto's struma) is associated with the use of iodized salt and other sources of dietary iodine, and (4) synthesis of labeled compounds for detection and treatment of neuroendocrine tumors and cholesterol analogues for imaging the adrenal.

Dr. Beierwaltes is currently Professor Emeritus, University of Michigan Medical Center.

When the University of Michigan put me on their committee to help select future "Distinguished Faculty Award" presentations, I decided that I would start using the *World's Who's Who in Science from Antiquity to the Present* for scientists, *Who's Who in America,* and *Who's Who in the World* as criteria in addition to workers in the university and elsewhere in their field. It disturbed me that I could only find the first edition of *Who's Who in Science from Antiquity to the Present*, which had been published in 1968. I called the Marquis Corporation and they explained to me that this effort to include the most important scientists from "antiquity to present" took a lot of outstanding personnel a very long time to compile. For example, the first two pages inside the cover list all the Nobel Prizes given from 1901 through 1967 under physics, chemistry, and physiology, or medicine. They explained that, since they almost went bankrupt producing this edition, they decided that they could not afford to do it again. It was a thrilling feeling to have been included in a write-up that included Newton, Galileo, and Nobel laureates.

Similarly, the AMA Scientific Achievement Award was accompanied by a piece of paper listing all the previous awardees since the award was started. I was thrilled by the relatively large number of Nobel Laureates in this list of thirty-three people since the award had been started in 1962.

Although the AMA award was given to me largely for the same reasons that Bill Kelly outlined above in my Distinguished Faculty Award, it was certainly precipitated at that particular time by the epochal announcement and presentation in *The New England Journal of Medicine* (the most distinguished medical journal in the world) of the successful treatment of non-Hodgkin's lymphoma with radio-iodinated antibodies and the subsequent discussion in the *Ann Arbor News* that led to Richard Wahl stressing that this publication was a direct result of the work that I had done beginning in 1940 to achieve this goal.

Travel—the Continued "Reward"

Fun at Meetings

One time when I was expressing my unhappiness with the comparatively poor salary I received from the University of Michigan in academic medicine, and even in private practice as compared to entertainers, one friend of mine said, "Bill, I think there is one thing that you are forgetting. Not because of the University of Michigan or the taxpayers of the State of Michigan paying you, but because the University of Michigan has offered a showcase for your abilities, it appears to me that you have had about a $20,000-a-year budget for travel for your entire career paid for by other institutions that wanted you as a speaker because of your current original work published in over three hundred publications and your constant series of lectures given elsewhere."

I had to agree that this was certainly a thrilling release from monotony supplied both to Mary-Martha and to me. When I first started at the University of Michigan with publications of original research work on the thyroid gland, the chairman of the

Department of Medicine made it clear that it was important to the University of Michigan that we present it at the annual fall meeting of the American Federation for Clinical Research and the Central Society for Clinical Research at the Drake Hotel in Chicago. Some money was even furnished by the chairman of the Department of Medicine for this purpose.

Similarly, it was an important function of the Department of Medicine to make certain that everyone doing research and publishing should go to the Atlantic City national meetings of the American Federation for Clinical Research, the American Society for Clinical Investigation, and the Association of American Physicians. These were particularly enjoyable because they opened a new life to me. Because my father had been a "legend in frugality," our lifestyle at home and even at Killarney and Aplin Beach was very modest, to say the least. The classrooms and laboratories and life as a teacher and researcher at the University of Michigan offered me the opportunity to live at exactly the same level as people associated with me in daily life who were much wealthier. I was particularly impressed at the Drake Hotel in Chicago.

One time they had warned me that the king and queen of England were coming there to stay while in Chicago, and the hotel had renovated an entire floor for them. It is only recently that I found out that the queen of England was the wealthiest woman in the world.

One time at the Drake Hotel we were put into a beautiful suite of rooms that had an open door to another beautiful suite. We went downstairs back to the manager of the hotel to remind him that we had asked for a guarantee of price for the cheapest room in the hotel. Although he was discreet, we found out later that we had received inadvertently the two suites of rooms set aside for Katherine Hepburn and her agent.

The second reason that these research meetings in the spring and fall were so wonderful was that we met all of the most important people in our field and were brought up to date ahead of all the journals by their presentations of the hottest and most recent developments in medicine (see appendix 3 for examples). A third reason was that we tended to eat at elegant restaurants, which we could not afford, with intelligent people who had a great sense of humor.

The meetings of the Association of American Physicians in Haddon Hall reminded me of King Arthur and his court.

At least one evening during the Atlantic City meetings each year, we would all congregate in Hackney's Seafood Restaurant. On the way into the restaurant, there were huge vats of circulating saltwater with hundreds of big lobsters from which you chose the lobster you wanted. I remember one time when we had a talented physician who knew how to pick them out of the vat and then stroke the underside of the lobster's belly to cause the lobster to go into a hypnotic trance so that the physician could lay the lobster on its back on top of the stainless steel side of the tank out of the water. The lobster would merely stay there in a trance without moving until the physician tapped the lobster the right way in the right place. Suddenly, the lobster was instantly alive and on the defensive and was tossed back into the tank.

Inside Hackney's Seafood Restaurant, there was a telephone at the central desk that would receive calls for doctors and other guests in the restaurant. Naturally, some young physicians thought up the trick of asking the poor clerk at this telephone to turn on the public address system to call very famous people in medicine who had existed before us and were now dead. Repeatedly, throughout the evening, the public address system would call us to attention for a message. "Will Sir William Osler please come to the telephone?" "Would Sir William Halstead please come to the telephone?" All the doctors "in the know" immediately burst out laughing hysterically, particularly to let other people know that they were on the inside of this joke.

Everyone tried to walk down the boardwalk to this restaurant, no matter how long the cocktail hour at the previous society meeting had lasted. The next show of endurance was to walk back after dinner. In the cases of the youngest and poorest, the only alternative was to take a Yellow Cab.

When I first went to these meetings, I tried to be very careful to choose the cheapest item on the menu or even order the cheapest thing when it was not on the menu, such as a hamburger (all I could possibly afford). The people in the know ordered very expensive things. When the meal was over, I found out that the routine ritual was to divide the bill equally for each one at that table to share equally, regardless of what they had ordered. This learning experience immediately changed my choice of food at this restaurant at future meetings.

As a person who had spent all of his life sailing, I particularly enjoyed the beautiful view of Lake Michigan from the Drake Hotel and the view of the Atlantic Ocean from Haddon Hall and Hackney's and the entire boardwalk. Needless to say, with the onset of gambling in Atlantic City, these meetings were moved to the best hotels in large cities in a rotating series of large cities with convention centers, art museums, etc. Another function of these meetings that I soon learned was to respond to any of the chairmen of departments who asked me if I planned to stay at the University of Michigan permanently or if I had ever considered moving. I learned to say, and also told my younger men to say, that I was always available to move elsewhere for a better opportunity but I had to have the exact position and the exact salary, etc., put in writing before I could even visit them. I would then present this written proposal to the chairman of my department, not stating that I would leave if he didn't beat it but merely to ask him what his thoughts were on this proposal.

I always remember that Bill Robinson told me that I was entirely out of reality when I asked for a certain salary and promotion. He stated that only surgeons could command such salaries. One proposal that I brought home from California was for a full professorship and a $35,000 increase in salary. Fifteen minutes after I had shown this proposal to Bill Robinson, I was walking to the main campus from the hospital when I ran into the vice president for finance of the University of Michigan who said, "Wow, that was some proposal that you got from that university in California." I said that I didn't know what he was talking about because the only proposal I had, I had given to the chairman of the Department of Medicine only fifteen minutes previously. He said, "That sort of news travels fast."

It seemed to me that all my promotions and pay raises at the University of Michigan came when I got a written offer to go elsewhere. Such letters are of great help to the division head or the department head trying to convince the administration that you are good enough and in enough demand by others outside the university that your university should respond if they want to keep good people. This doesn't mean that they are asking the university to furnish the money, merely that they're asking that the division head or department chairman be allowed to pay your salary, even if it comes out of your own grants to you directly from the National Institutes of Health or the Atomic Energy Commission, etc.

My wife reminds me that I was a good father but that the majority of requests to go elsewhere to lecture came for the spring season. This was strikingly true and we used the expression, "In the spring the knights go forth to do battle."

It is impossible for us to match the kind of travel that we had then when we now pay for that travel ourselves and do it on our own rather than by request of somebody who lives where you want to go.

The international thyroid meetings in London and Rome, for example, could not be equalled, primarily because the people in London cared for royalty in their practice and knew all the most important people and all the best places to go. We had one banquet for husbands and wives in London under the auspices of the Lord Mayor's House. The waiters were dressed in outstanding classical costumes. One of them slapped the wrist of the woman sitting next to me, who was the wife of a distinguished American thyroidologist, because she started to light a cigarette before we had "the toast to the queen." Every evening in Rome, we had a cocktail party and hors d'oeuvres and/or dinner in one of the most outstanding classical institutions in Rome. Over a period of time, we thus visited in great depth seven out of the eight most outstanding art museums in the world.

Hawaii

Perhaps my wife's fondest memories are of our fabulous, two-week lectureship in the Hawaiian Islands. It started with a phone call to me from the head of Nuclear Medicine in the

129

biggest medical clinic in the Hawaiian Islands. He made it clear that this was not an invitation but merely a question to find out whether I could possibly be free the following spring for two weeks with my wife if I were invited with no honorarium but with all expenses paid for her and me to a hotel of my choice in Oahu on the beach to give a one-hour lecture each morning, five days a week, to physicians on the subject of nuclear medicine. He stressed that each year the Hawaiian Island Medical Society decided on a topic, and they had chosen nuclear medicine for that year. They were, therefore, going to consult the so-called top nuclear medicine leaders to find out whether they were interested and available.

Just as my wife had about given up, I received a phone call in February of the following year stating that I had been selected. I was told to go to my travel agent and complete the travel arrangements to and from there and to select my own hotel. The woman at the travel agency selected a modest but good hotel on the beach.

It turned out that the overall president of all the medical societies was an M.D., Ted Tomita, who had graduated from the University of Michigan Medical School and was practicing in Oahu and had been campaign manager for the mayor of the town as well as the governor of the state, and was now president of the Hawaiian Medical Societies. Ted Tomita and his wife met us at the plane, put leis around our necks, and took us to our hotel. He told me that the chief of nuclear medicine at the clinic would pick me up at the hotel at 7:00 A.M. and we would have breakfast there overlooking the ocean. He would then take me downtown to lecture in a large auditorium for one hour. Ted would then bring me back to my hotel where we would pick up Mary-Martha, and in our informal "Hawaiian clothes," we would take a tour, which included lunch at the restaurant of one of his patients. He would then take us back to the hotel and make it clear that no further demands would be put upon our time. He gave us the keys to the car and maps for where we might like to go.

We said good-bye and went up to our hotel room. It was late, at the time of sunset. I walked onto the back porch overlooking the beach and the ocean. I almost instantly yelled at Mary-

Martha to come to see the couple dancing under a big palm tree directly behind our hotel between the hotel and the shore. There was a fairly large number of native Hawaiians watching this couple. I told Mary-Martha, "I don't know who these people are or what they're doing, but this is the most incredible dancing I've ever seen in my life. Come quickly." She came and watched and agreed completely. Several days later, we were guests at the number one hotel at the number one floor show in Oahu. The same couple were the lead dancers in the floor show. Our hosts informed us that the palm tree was an ancient tree and the dancing around the tree had first been carried out ages ago. It was traditional for the competitors in this competition for the best dancers in Hawaii to dance around that tree on that particular day of that month each year. The couple we had seen dancing that night won the contest as the best dancers in Hawaii.

Ted and his wife were very careful never to suggest that we had to do anything that they were doing socially. They merely told us what they were doing in case we wanted to come. It seemed to me that the next night we had dinner in the Officers Club at sunset overlooking the ocean. It was fabulous. After two days of lecture in Oahu, we were flown to another Hawaiian island for me to lecture for one hour there.

I remember the day that we flew to Maui. I looked for someone to pick us up, but apparently no one was there. As we were about to get public transportation, a very nice woman came up to me and said, "By any chance, could you be Dr. Beierwaltes?" and I said yes. She said she had come to pick up her sister, but her sister had not appeared. She wanted me to know that we did not have to come with her but she was driving back into town if we wanted a ride. Of course, we took the ride. On the way there, she asked us if we had been to see the inactive volcano that was so famous. She made it clear that we didn't have to go there, but it was a popular thing to do in case we were interested. Of course, we did.

She then said that her husband was president of that county's medical society and had said something about me lecturing that night. She therefore took us to our hotel. Before dropping us off, she said that she and her husband had one of the most outstanding dancers in the Hawaiian islands performing at a dinner party that they were having that evening for friends. She made it clear that we were not required to come but, if we cared to, they would be delighted to have us. Of course, we went.

The next day at each of these islands we were given the key to a car and maps on where to go and what to see. We would drive around and then return. After a few days, Mary-Martha said, "Bill, do you realize that we are being entertained?" I said, "Yes, I now do but it is subtle!"

For example, somehow they learned that I was a small boat sailor and was crazy about thistles and that my wife and her family were all "Yale." That evening the doctor sitting next to me at dinner was captain of the thistle fleet on Oahu, and the doctor sitting next to my wife was not only from Yale but his grandfather had come from Yale as a missionary. We had read James Michener's *Hawaii* in preparation for the trip, and so it was fun to go through all the details with him. The statement was made that the missionaries came to the Hawaiian Islands to do good and they did very well indeed.

A few years later when we dropped into the Hawaiian Islands on our way back from Japan, we experienced no thrill for the simple reason that we did not have every doctor in the Hawaiian Islands trying to make our visit spectacular and enjoyable.

Baghdad

September, 1963, I accepted a job for AID in Baghdad for twenty-one days because they paid me the top consulting salary of $100 a day and I suddenly found that I needed $2,100 to pay our oldest son's first-year tuition starting at Kalamazoo College.

Typical of what I have just talked about is my trip from Baghdad to Mosul. I was given plane tickets to leave Baghdad one day to lecture in Mosul. When I came to the airport, I stood in line. An obvious official in the airport singled me out of line and told me that I did not need to have a seat assignment or baggage check-in. He suggested that I come with him to another large room in the airport, where he introduced me to the dean of the medical school in Mosul. They noticed that I was concerned about getting the right plane at the right time to get there and told me to relax because the man who had singled me out of line was the director of the airport and "no plane takes off until he says it can."

The temperature in Baghdad at that time of year reached 110 to 120° F. and the humidity was practically 0 percent. Practically all beer sold was in half-gallon bottles. I reluctantly accepted a bottle of beer because my hosts were drinking one also. I realized that the time for the departure of our plane, which was British Airways, had arrived early in hitting the bottle. As we were nearing the end of drinking our beer they asked me why I was so fidgety. I explained to them that the time of departure of our plane had passed about twenty minutes ago. They reminded me that the plane did not take off until the director said it could. We therefore leisurely walked out on the field, and there was the plane loaded with passengers for the last half hour awaiting my triumphal entrance with the director of the airport and the dean of the medical school in Mosul.

Mexico

Lastly, there was an International Society of Nuclear Medicine meeting in Mexico. Naturally, everyone thinks of going to Acapulco. No, this was in an exclusive place that people outside Mexico had seldom heard about. It was at the Hacienda Vista Hermosa in Morelos. This is a former palace of Hernando Cortez, the Spanish conquistador who defeated the Aztec empire. He built a palace of Hacienda Vista Hermosa in Morelos about 1518. We were there in these magnificent ruins. Our hotel room was about sixty feet long, fifteen feet wide, and about twenty-five feet high. It had originally been used to store sugar. Each window had a window seat because the walls were about three feet thick. The door was a very heavy wooden door and required a large steel key to open it. There was a huge outdoor swimming pool that was fed by an aqueduct about fifteen to twenty feet above the pool, with the water coming down into the pool from a hole in the wall of the aqueduct. The dining room was about two hundred feet long and one hundred feet wide and the walls were about sixty feet high. About one-third of the roof at one end had caved in and that furnished the light.

Only bumpy, muddy roads led into the Hacienda Vista Hermosa. Our hosts more or less implied that this is purposeful to keep out all but dedicated visitors to the Hacienda Vista Hermosa.

There was a small town (Cuernavaca) about fifteen miles from Morelos where we were taken to a unique dinner. There was a private house whose front porch was not more than seven feet from the street. The back yard of the house, however, was almost an acre in size. There were rattan tables and chairs on the back lawn. Next to each table was the equivalent of an artist's easel. The waitress would bring a large card to set on the easel that showed what drinks were available and their cost. After this, she brought out another card and, with fluorescent paint to be seen in the dark, presented the menu choices for each course.

During the evening, there were large pink flamingos walking freely around the various tables, not to compete with you in eating your food but to keep the lawn clean in case you should drip any food. This was a delightful experience.

Many people asked me why I didn't quit all medicine as soon as I retired from the University of Michigan seven years ago. They thought the main thing I should do was travel. I explained to them, "TRAVEL?!"

I explained to them that I had to travel all my life as part of my work. The invention of the compound that treated the tumors of the adrenal medulla and neuroblastomas was accompanied by an acceleration of these travels. We were asked to travel to Italy several times in one six-month period because companies there were interested in leasing or buying our patents on this compound and had me lecture.

On one of the visits, one of my past trainees, who was head of nuclear medicine at Udine, Italy, staged an "international" meeting for me in Udine. I was to be given a key to the town at six o'clock at a banquet, etc. We started out two and a half hours late from Detroit Metropolitan Airport because of Pan Am's problems. This ended with us spending thirteen hours in airports in England and Italy. We got in at twelve o'clock at night, and one of my trainees asked us if we needed any food and handed me the key to the town that the mayor had left when he went home.

Mary-Martha asked me if this was what I thought was most fun in life, and I said that it just occurred to me that it was time for us to cut out 99 percent of all travel.

The Extended Family

Friday, December 2, 1994, Mary-Martha and I attended, by invitation of David Kuhl, the annual Christmas party of the University of Michigan Clinical Nuclear Medicine Division.

It was held in the Holiday Inn on the North Campus of the University of Michigan. Suddenly, I realized the heritage that my efforts in starting a new specialty in medicine, that of nuclear medicine, had produced.

On page 408 of my first book for doctors, *The Clinical Use of Radioactive Isotopes*, the statement of space gives a brief objective statement of the program of just space requirements. "Since 1947, our isotope unit has grown, from a Geiger counter and an early model scaler with no room to put them in, to one room in 1949, 1,000 square feet of floor space in 1951, and to 3,800 square feet of floor space in 1956, with many thousands of dollars worth of equipment."

When we moved into the new University of Michigan Hospital in 1987, we had 10,000 square feet of floor space in the clinical unit, and about 36,000 square feet of research space in three buildings, and a total budget of about eight million dollars a year, mostly self-generated by research grants and income from patient service.

When we walked into the ballroom dining room at the Holiday Inn for the annual Christmas party of the Division of Nuclear Medicine of the University Hospital, Ann Arbor, I counted thirty round tables, seating eight people each. When Dave Kuhl, my successor as chief of the Nuclear Medicine Division, presented remarks on the health of the Nuclear Medicine

Division in 1994, he pointed out that the division had 134 employees, 20,000 square feet of clinical space, 40,000 square feet of research space, and six million dollars in research grants.

He itemized five doctors who had achieved recognition in the 1994–95 edition of *The Best Doctors in America* and numerous well-known research recognition awards.

Most touching to me was the fact that one of the Ph.D.s in physics that I had brought in, Les Rogers, had just had his grant titled, "Radiation Detection and Quantification," re-awarded in a *very* competitive field. This re-award had given him a total of twenty consecutive years with this grant that I had thought up with his help and with the help of Glenn Knoll, a Ph.D. in electrical engineering. I remember that Glenn Knoll had criticized my title of "Radiation Detection and Quantification" on the original grant but couldn't think up a better title.

Before I left the university in 1987, Glenn had published an outstanding textbook, titled *Radiation Detection and Quantification*, and had shortly after that been promoted to a full professor of nuclear engineering. Last month he was asked to be dean of the School of Engineering.

It occurred to me that I had been given a silver bowl with names and years of service of eighty-eight of my physician trainees who had trained a minimum of two years with me. I had additional trainees from almost every country in the world. One year one of my trainees, Howard Dworkin, was president of the United States Society of Nuclear Medicine. Another one of my trainees, Tom Haney, M.D., was editor of the *Journal of Nuclear Medicine*. My ex-radiation health physicist, Audrey Wegst, Ph.D.; my trainee from Alexandria, Egypt, Dr. Mohammad Nofal; and my trainee from Bombay, India, Rahman Ganatra, M.D. were running the Nuclear Medicine Division of the World Atomic Energy Commission in Vienna, Austria. Lionel Lieberman, M.D. and David Woodbury, M.D. were staffing the Radiopharmaceutical Division of the United States Food and Drug Administration with another one of my trainees, Eric Jones.

One of my men, Jim Thrall, became chairman of the Department of Radiology at Massachusetts General Hospital in

Boston and took many of my younger men with him.

It occurred to me at the University of Michigan Christmas party that I had spent many wonderful hours with this extended family—all of them (and many more!)—being a role model for them and daily encouraging them to publish, to go to research meetings, and to get grants showing them off at research meetings. I reminded them that we had developed a Camelot at the University of Michigan and a new specialty of medicine devoted to caring for the sick directly and indirectly. Directly through one-on-one diagnosis and treatment, less directly by teaching, and most indirectly but most widely by inventing new methods of diagnosis and treatment of patients through medical research for others to use all over the world.

In prospect, during, and in retrospect, it perhaps is now my greatest thrill to see them launched into such a productive and rewarding life.

My Beloved

First Love—
Mother and Father

I would agree with the current literature that says that, as soon as a baby is able to distinguish others from himself, his first bonding hopefully is with his parents, siblings, and grandparents. My first memories of my mother and father are recorded at the outset of this book.

My experience as a child, parent, and now a grandparent confirms that ideally the young child appreciates having each new acquaintance devote 100 percent of his/her time to the child while in the child's presence. If the parent has the audacity to pick up a newspaper to read in the child's presence, the child slaps it down and makes it clear that he or she will not tolerate this shabby treatment.

Similarly, as a grandparent, I now know that grandchildren automatically grade grandparents. If the grandparent is eager (or even willing) to devote 100 percent of his/her time to being attentive to the grandchild, that grandparent gets an "A."

As a grandparent, my father was sensational with our children for up to an hour of entertaining. He would sing little songs, pull coins out of their ears and nose, etc.

As a parent witnessing my father at work with our children, I was impressed that my father would then imply that it was now time for the parent to "take them away." I looked forward to the day when I, as a grandparent, could say (or imply without words), "Take them away."

Our latest grandchild, Nora Rose, a fabulous granddaughter, at the age of one taught me that I rated an "A" to devote full time to her needs when she started to yell at the table when she had finished eating before the rest of us. Her needs were first and foremost to ritualistically point to a shelf and grunt at me that she wanted each of three "snow globes" turned upside down, one after another, to let her wind up the sound and then let the snow gather in the "top" of the inverted water-filled glass globe. I was then to right it and listen to the sound as the snow fell. Most importantly, she then showed great recognition of the value of her grandfather when she saw her grandfather rather firmly stop her brothers, Peter and Willy, from teasing her ultimately by standing one in front of her and one in back of her and kicking the fairly large soccer ball past her out of her reach when she wanted to participate in this play. They smiled and enjoyed themselves most when she screamed and cried.

As our children matured, I realized that my father was an ardent and excellent teaser. I then realized that he had unwittingly taught me how to tease others, particularly my brother Jack. I realized that I had mercilessly teased Jack. At least on one occasion, I escaped severe punishment by outrunning Jack in front of the cottages at Killarney Beach on Saginaw Bay as he chased me down the beach after I had ruined his supper with my teasing. I never realized how my father had teased me and my brother Jack until I saw my father pitting our sons Willie and Andy against each other by teasing.

I also remember how sexually attractive my mother was to me as a woman and her excited look as she would come down the stairway in the cottage with a new outfit on and a new hairdo to show us. I also remember how fascinated I was with her knowledge from reading the latest *Reader's Digest*, etc.

My memory of my mother and father as role models of married parents was that Dad was always hugging and kissing my mother with considerable feeling in front of us until he got into his sixties.

It was also of interest to me that they began to have lots of arguments and rarely hugged and kissed as they got into their sixties. It was of great interest to me that Dad's favorite term of endearment for my mother was to refer to her as "Mary Pickford." It became obvious to me that Mary Pickford was "America's sweetheart" and wife to Douglas Fairbanks Sr. and thus Dad was paying my mother a great compliment by calling her "Mary Pickford" to express how beautiful and exciting he thought she was.

It was also of great interest to me that my parents excused Jack and me from the table after dinner and then they talked together about life for another half hour to an hour, thus making it easier for them to talk about their current problems and solutions in life without monitoring their words in the presence of their children.

It is also of great interest to me that my father explained to us that, just because Mother prepared the meal, this did not mean that she should have to wash the dishes. He, therefore, participated with us in clearing the table and washing the dishes every evening until he was convinced that we could do it without his help. It is of interest to me that I continued to do this as a dishwasher at Gamma Phi Beta sorority while in college until I became a waiter and then later adopted this as a policy in my home with my own children.

I was also very impressed that, when my mother developed congestive heart failure at age seventy-six, before she died of a stroke, my father had Uncle Honus build her a downstairs bedroom extension to our living room on the first floor so that she would not have to walk up and down the stairs. He was also delighted to wait on her "hand and foot" twenty-four hours a day as necessary since he had retired from his job at age seventy-three.

Our children have recently told Mary-Martha and me that they remember with strongly positive feelings our role model in taking Dad into our home to live with us when he was eighty-four years of age. They were impressed at how much we liked Dad (with a shared sense of humor about his developing infirmities) and how much he enjoyed going with us in our cars, no matter where we went.

Our children also thrilled at us taking him abroad for the first time in his life (at age eighty-two) to the International Thyroid Meeting in Rome and then to see our cousins in Germany for the first time.

Recently, Will, Marty, and Andy told me how they want to emulate this behavior with us. They also would rather see us enjoy spending our money on ourselves rather than making that big effort to pass it all on to them.

Childhood Sweethearts

I have mentioned some of my childhood sweethearts in my chapter on the seventh grade titled, "My First Date." I also covered my social development from seventh grade through high school. The entire emphasis was to have a party of friends at each other's house for a party on a weekly basis to socialize and dance. I described the Saginaw Auditorium and the weekly big-name bands.

The emphasis here was to gradually learn how much fun it was to talk and kiss and hug ("pet") one's latest girlfriend and enjoy the social events together.

Our parents had thoroughly informed us of *all* the hazards of extramarital sexual intercourse, and I'm glad that I never indulged in it. A strong motivation to stay virginal was that having a child would mean that I would have to give up my passion for going into medicine while working to pay most of my expenses to get seven years of formal course work at the University of Michigan.

We were also impressed with the terrible potentials of gonorrhea and central nervous system syphilis. There were no sulfas or penicillins to treat infectious diseases at that time.

I also remember that I thoroughly enjoyed the company of every girl I dated, some more than others, primarily based on their sense of humor and their ability to dance.

Only two or three girls excited me sexually enough to spend the evening petting.

Phyllis Sterling was the most compatible and enjoyable person I dated, but something told me I should continue to look before I married because in theory I would meet someone who would thoroughly stir my passions.

As head waiter at Delta Tau Delta fraternity at the University of Michigan 1938–39, I admired a healthy-looking, social

144

"big woman on campus" that our house manager, Beezie, brought to parties at the house. I announced to my fellow waiters and dishwashers that they should look at her because I had decided that she had the appearance and presence of the type of girl that I had decided I wanted to marry.

Mary-Martha Nichols

The next Friday, we had a Phi Chi medical fraternity house party and an undergrad from Detroit named Arman Darmstetter brought with him a girl named Mary-Martha Nichols from New Haven, Connecticut. I took one look at her and made a decision then that I would marry her. I spent the evening trying to impress her. I showed her my bones from my anatomy course and talked to her every minute I could that evening. The next morning I called her to further develop the acquaintance and she could not remember anything about me. I finally asked her whether she did or did not remember attending the party at the Phi Chi house. She did remember that but not me!

I Pursue Her

I finally convinced Mary-Martha that she should have a date with me. Her father was chairman of the botany department at Yale University and had taught at the University of Michigan biological station since 1920. Later she told me that, when I called her on the telephone, she first assumed I was one of his former students who wanted a date and she was not enthusiastic about dating her father's students. I then found that she was signed up for dates weeks in advance, and I decided to launch a campaign to attract her interest. I invited one of my best friends, Bob Leach, who was also a waiter at Delta Tau Delta and a medical fraternity brother, to get a date with her roommate, Harriet Heames. Bob was very handsome and had a great sense of humor. Bob and Harriet were to double-date with me and my latest, most beautiful date of the month. Harriet would then go home and tell her roommate, Mary-Martha, all about what had happened.

146

One time, while walking home from a University of Michigan basketball game, Mary-Martha passed me while my very attractive date and I were wrestling in the snow. I was wrestling with my date to get the snowballs away from her that she had been throwing at me.

Another time, we just happened to dance near Mary-Martha and her date at a dance at an intimate small restaurant in Ann Arbor after Bob Leach had informed me that Mary-Martha was going to be there.

Finally, on one of my dates with Mary-Martha, which I had signed up for weeks in advance, I complained to her that it was *very* hard for me to have to sign up so long in advance for a date. She suddenly produced her date book and asked me to fill in any dates I wanted.

She now explains my success in trying to attract her with one of her usual parsimonious answers: "He tried and tried to attract me until I finally caught him."

Unfortunately, my sophomore year of medical school was at that time the most demanding and I was head waiter at Delta Tau Delta. I was so passionately in love with her that, when I was with her, I was in heaven. Although she was willing to study at the library with me a lot, when I told her I would have to take a day off to study alone, I found that I was miserable and called her to rectify this dilemma. We also remember my trying to impress her at a picnic near Barton Dam on the Huron River by my doing gymnastics that I had learned from my father and from being on the University of Michigan gym team in 1934–37.

We also remember staying out canoeing later than her dormitory, Helen Newberry, allowed without penalty. The penalty was an earlier curfew on her next date.

We bared our souls to each other in long, wonderful conversations that helped us get further acquainted.

She invited me to her home in New Haven, Connecticut, for Christmas vacation. We went to the Yale Law School annual Christmas dance the first night I was there. As soon as we started to dance, I was "cut in on." Instantly, I cut in on the couple next to me. The girl was from the Hawaiian Islands and was going to the Katherine Gibbs School in Boston. Like me, she had never been to New Haven before and, of course, had never been to the law school annual Christmas dance. She said that her roommate was from the University of Michigan, and she wondered if I knew her. I said that it was *very* unlikely since there were thousands of students at the University of Michigan. *Much to our surprise*, her roommate was the girlfriend of my roommate, John Bricker!

Mary-Martha Goes to Pratt Institute

Mary-Martha's father died at the end of my sophomore year (1938), and she decided to stay closer to her mother that year and go to Pratt Institute in Brooklyn rather than return to art school at the University of Michigan. She was there for only one semester and then left Pratt to take a job in New Haven to be even closer to her mother.

She had skipped her first year at Yale Art School by showing the portfolio that she had acquired from her private art instructress, who had a master's degree from the Yale Art School. After her first semester at Yale, she got a scholarship based on academic excellence for the following semester.

I also found out that most art students who are accepted at Pratt Institute have almost a straight-A average. For commercial art, a degree from Pratt was like a master's degree in business administration from Harvard in the business world.

While in high school, Mary-Martha had won first prize in a city-wide contest for a poster for a charity drive. She and a partner had also won a contest for the best window decoration of Malley's Department Store. She could easily have had a career in fashion design if she had finished her degree at Pratt and probably would have if her father had lived and continued to encourage her.

At any rate, we decided to get married, but Mary-Martha thought it wise to wait until I had at least started my internship. We then had the agreement that we should both be free to date other people until we were married.

In the chapter entitled, "Retrospect: The Ecstasies," I have outlined the wonderful time I had during my internship before she came to Cleveland as my wife.

We Marry

We finally set the date for the wedding as January 1, 1942. Since I was being paid nothing for my internship at Cleveland Metropolitan Hospital, I donated three blood transfusions to earn $75 ($25 each) to pay for my round-trip train fare from Cleveland to New Haven and hopefully for an overnight honeymoon at the Roosevelt Hotel in New York City. I chose the Roosevelt Hotel because it was in the train station, which meant we would not have to pay for a taxicab to the hotel and back.

Our wedding was at Mary-Martha's Baptist church in New Haven. Later, that church was purchased by Yale University and converted into a theater building for their School of Drama.

Our room at the Roosevelt Hotel was okay except that the thermometer in the room was stuck at about 85 degrees for the night. The cliché was that this resulted in "a hot time in the old town tonight!" The next morning we took the coach to Cleveland and spent a week, more or less, in bed in our tiny apartment.

Our apartment cost us a dollar a day! We shared the bathroom on our floor with another couple and a single man who apparently got drunk and very nauseated every night and vomited in our communal bathtub. Nevertheless, we were so madly in love that we rarely got out of bed for several days and could not imagine a more intimate honeymoon even if we could have afforded it.

Mary-Martha first got a job working for the dean of the Cleveland Metropolitan Hospital Department of Nursing. Then, she got a much higher paying job with Jones and Laughlin Steel, located behind the hospital in the Cuyahoga Valley. We did not find out until a year later how dangerous her walk was to and from work at Jones and Laughlin.

One Year in Bed with Tuberculosis

Two and a half months after we were *very happily married*, it was discovered that I had bilateral minimal pulmonary tuberculosis and I was put to bed in the Lowman Memorial Tuberculosis Sanitarium of Cleveland Metropolitan Hospital for an unknown period of time, which turned out to be one year. INH and PAS had just been approved for treatment of tuberculosis in the military only because of the war effort. (This was soon after the Japanese attack on Pearl Harbor on December 7, 1941.)

As I relate in the chapter, "Medicine," I was then started on an artificial pneumothorax to rest my right lung and had to have air refills once a week. My pneumothorax was abandoned five and a half years later. I therefore had an "acute anxiety state" for five and a half years, which was very hard on both of us and our first child, Andy.

We Return to Ann Arbor

Under "Medicine" I relate how I was accepted back at the University of Michigan Hospital for completion of my residency in internal medicine. Mary-Martha went to Ann Arbor to find a home for us and secured a huge house from Mrs. Pendergrass, a wonderful widow, who primarily needed a caretaker for the house and charged us a token forty dollars a month to cover the cost of the heat only because we insisted on paying something. Mrs. Pendergrass was the widow of an English professor at the University of Michigan. Two months later, when we were able to find an apartment on "Poverty Row" three blocks from the hospital and moved there, Mrs. Pendergrass came to return some objects that we had left in her house and to chat with Mary-Martha. It was either one or two weeks later we found out she had committed suicide by jumping out of the window of her room in the Waldorf-Astoria in New York City. Her house was luxurious beyond our fondest dreams but was filled with loud and varied sounds all night long seven nights a week. We eventually gave up investigating these causes all night long.

Eras of Our Life

The Era of Cannon's Castle on Poverty Row

Mary-Martha got a job with Willard Olson, a professor of education, only a few blocks from our house. She then "got the hots" for having children and getting a house. Suddenly, all rationale related to my earning $600 a year disappeared. (My favorite daughter-in-law showed me by example that this is a common development in young married women.)

Andy was born April 22, 1945, while we lived in a tiny apartment in Mr. Cannon's house across from the School of Public Health and two blocks from the front of the University Hospital on "Poverty Row." He was delivered by Pat Haas, an outstanding obstetrics professor under Norman Miller, and a patient of mine. When he walked in to attend the delivery, he found that Andy was in frank breech position and had a prolapsed umbilical cord as well as a nuchal arm (behind the neck) requiring Dührsen's incisions to get the baby out. Each of these complications *alone* in previous deliveries at University Hospital had been fatal. We believe that perhaps the complications contributed to the production of our final diagnosis of dyslexia (which no one knew about at that time).

Our principal recreation with our friends was to grow a vegetable garden as part of the war effort in an empty lot next to the School of Public Health in front of our houses along that street.

We were told that if we did not have a private income we should not go into academic medicine.

My chief, Dr. Sturgis, commanded a salary of $10,000 a year at the University of Michigan, but I always was impressed when J. C. Penney was his private patient. Dr. Sturgis charged Mr. Penney $1,500 every time he walked into his hospital room. He

151

used to say, "Beierwaltes, I know you live in poverty, but it is *genteel* poverty!"

It still is impressive to young doctors to learn, however, that after working my way through seven years of college with no debts to pay off, Mary-Martha and I could not purchase a car until we had been married for five and a half years and I had my M.D. degree for that five and a half years.

"Poverty Row" (Washington Heights) was parallel to the front of the University of Michigan Hospital and one block away from the side of the School of Public Health. Our apartment cost us $35 a month. It had a bathroom and our bed was in a butler's pantry. We also had a living room with a closet and a small kitchen. Mary-Martha and I could both walk to our respective jobs.

One of the highlights of that time was my evening conversation on the way home on the front steps of the School of Public Health with Jonas Salk, who later practically eliminated poliomyelitis from the surface of the earth. The conversation was usually dominated by Jonas's anxiety about whether or not his old secondhand car would start and get him home that evening. We have been good friends ever since.

During my rest hours at home, I wrote three essays emphasizing how important it is to have a sense of humor to carry one through such periods. I never submitted them for publication but include them now, as written fifty years ago to give you a taste of our sense of humor while living in Poverty Row!

English Instructor

Our landlord had once been an instructor in English at a Midwestern agricultural college. When we first heard about this upon moving into our new apartment, we were quite pleased that we had landed such an illustrious landlord. It soon turned out, however, that on the contrary, our landlord had landed a pupil. It was hard to explain his desire to educate other people. I don't think he really thought we were illiterate. It was probably that he just got so much enjoyment out of his own reading that he wanted us and everyone else to read everything he did.

I say everyone else because when we became confidential with our minister, assistant minister, and even a few other members of the congregation, they all gladly confessed that he had been in the habit for as long as they could remember of clipping articles out of papers and magazines in great profusion and distributing them to all these supposedly fortunate people. He apparently was a very prolific clipper, judging from the great number of people that were on his personal list, and I imagine that one of the functions of his basement was to act as a collecting depot, or poor man's library, for the sources of these clippings. Indeed, if you were really dear to him, he would just bring the whole magazine, or several of them, right to you personally. Once when my wife was ill, he "dropped in a little reading matter" for her, including a tangy basement copy of a 1929 *Harper's Bazaar*.

We had not enjoyed our new residence long before Mr. Cannon started a systematic plan of reading—for me. This program started insidiously enough with, "I have a few articles in this *Atlantic Monthly* that I am sure you would be interested in reading. As soon as you are through, let me know so that I can let some other friends of mine read it." This was my first deadline.

The next evening Mr. Cannon came in to quiz me on my reading. He was not the least chagrined to find that I had not yet opened or looked at the magazine. "That's all right, take your time and I'll be back for it tomorrow night." Being very naive at this stage of the game, I thought perhaps that if the articles were dutifully scanned that evening I could pass the quiz the next evening and have the whole situation dismissed so that I could get back to my necessary medical reading. How wrong that hope was! Since I passed the quiz, even though with a rather low grade, the next evening, it was apparently decided that I had now finished the preliminaries. Therefore when the first magazine was returned, my reward was the previous six months' issues of the *Atlantic Monthly*. The articles to be read were all given a preliminary verbal review by my self-appointed educator to stimulate my interest, which even he must have

153

suspected was showing visible signs of flagging. Actually, I knew it was not flagging but had just not started.

This large stock of reading material was neatly piled in the corner until I could get up enough nerve to tell my mentor that I had no time to read them even if I had the interest, which I didn't. After stopping in for a few minutes each evening to make a brief check on my progress, Mr. Cannon decided that my trouble was a lack of quantity. He then brought me the issues antedating by twelve successive months the ones I had stacked in the corner. This act staggered and stunned me to silence. About the time I had decided upon the plan of just leaving them in two's and three's at his front door on the way to work in the morning in a very stealthy manner so that I would escape the dreaded quiz, Mr. Cannon blew in one evening with a book written by one of his more illustrious relatives (Allison Ind, his son-in-law, was the author of the best seller, *Bataan, the Judgment Seat*).

A few days later, while my wife was ill and confined to the hospital, I retired very early in the evening to get a much needed rest. When I had just started to dream of Mr. Cannon sitting in a huge steam shovel dumping carloads of magazines out of a library reading room right into my well-stacked corner and completely filling our little apartment, I was suddenly awakened by a loud booming voice saying, "How are you coming on that book?"

"Wha—ho—who—oh, it's you, Mr. Cannon." He had walked into the apartment in his usual informal manner, turned on the light, and sighted me in bed. "Why, I haven't had time. . ."

"Oh, is that right? Well, I'll tell you what I'll do. I'll find a place for you to start. If you start out there and read the rest of the book, you will get the crux of the whole matter. Where is the book?"

With this I answered my cue by very sleepily climbing out of bed in my pajamas and finding the book for him through mere slits of eyes.

"Oh yes. Well, let me see." He then proceeded to thoughtfully turn the pages. It soon became apparent to me that he would become quite interested in every other page and read it through to refresh his memory of the matter while I sleepily

154

stood at his side with poorly faked interest. After the first twenty pages, I felt my friend Sleep slowly taking me away from this horrible reality.

"If you don't mind, Mr. Cannon, I think I will climb back into bed. When you find the place, just leave the book on the table and I will take it up in the morning."

"That's right. Don't let me interfere with your sleep. You go to bed and get a good sleep."

With that I rapidly fell off into my dreams. I was soon to find that my destiny was not to be so sweet, for no sooner had I dropped off into this enviable state than I was startled with a mighty blast from my literate tormentor, "Here it is, I found it. Here is the place. Well, you just read on from here and I guess that will take care of it all right."

Perhaps I should leave the story of the English instructor at this point, but someone might get the idea that I did not have spine enough to call this state of affairs to a halt. Well, I didn't. My mother-in-law visited us shortly thereafter. He immediately gave her a book to read. We hated to see her meet the same horrible fate. I pictured her in a few days seated in the living room chair surrounded by books and issues of *Atlantic Monthly* with Mr. Cannon frantically struggling up and down his favorite basement stairs with his arms loaded with magazines and books for my mother-in-law. This was too much to even consider. We tipped her off as to what might eventually happen to her.

She ended the whole matter immediately by having Mr. Cannon clean out our apartment of its books and magazines. She also told him in gentle but firm language that we never had time to read anything that we weren't already reading when we moved to his apartment house and that. . . .

Well, we haven't been troubled quite so much lately.

The Grandson

Most of our landlord's relatives were not the average cats. You couldn't really say they were insane. Only his youngest daughter was actually hospitalized for a while in a state institution. The rest of the relatives never quite made it.

155

Take our landlord's grandson, Stanley. For a while he reacted very peculiarly indeed.

It came to us more or less as a surprise. We never suspected that anything unusual had happened to Stanley because he always acted as though a few rather large areas of his frontal cortex had failed to develop. Oh, there had been a couple of incidents lately that were even more bizarre than usual.

Stanley was our paper boy. One Saturday afternoon I had just finished vacuuming the living room rug when Stanley came in to collect for the paper. He was a tall, lanky, awkward, fourteen-year-old boy with his first blush of adolescent acne on his soft whiskered face. When we finally found the little red newspaper score card, Stanley obligingly punched it as he stood quietly ill at ease in the middle of my just cleaned rug. As the paper punch grated through the unfortunate score card, a horrible little shower of punched paper from other cards floated down over a large area to rest upon my rug.

"Stanley," I said, with some choke in my voice, "the next time you punch our card, I wonder if you would mind stepping outside in the hall or using a wastebasket. I just finished cleaning the rug."

"Yes, sir," he said as he shifted uneasily over to a different section of the clean rug. There he nervously batted the paper punch against his other palm while we both looked on rather discouraged as a new and much larger shower of paper descended upon my formerly cleaned rug. Stanley finally looked up, gave me another vacant smile, and ambled out the door, while I just sat there smoking my pipe, contemplating the relative merits of euthanasia.

Another incident also should have made us somewhat suspicious that something had happened to the grandson that had made his behavior even more aberrant than usual. My wife had retired to a spare room at my request so that she might get some much-needed rest before we went out for the evening. Fortunately, she had not undressed before she lay down to sleep. For no sooner had she started to drowse off than the door opened and Stanley looked in with one of his winning vacant smiles.

"I'm in here sleeping," my wife said since she knew that all

156

situations needed explanation to Stanley.

"Oh well, then, it's all right. Come on in, Joe," he said to an invisible friend out in the hall. With this introduction, in walked both of these sterling examples of delayed maturation with a very full newspaper bag. This bag contained all the newspapers that Stanley's patient customers had been waiting for an hour or so. It seemed that Stanley had been preparing labels of his own to paste on each paper in order to advertise a book that his father had just published. While my wife writhed about on the bed in silent but horrifying contemplation, Stanley and his assistant advertiser happily pasted labels onto the papers, which read, "It's terrific, it's a sensation, read Allison Ind's new best seller, *Bataan, the Judgment Seat*."

There were other little things that should have made us suspicious that something unusual had happened to the grandson. He had missed us several times on his route in the past. But recently the incidence of these omissions had increased. His mother was besieged by calls from irate customers. One night I asked Mr. Cannon if he thought it was worthwhile for me to try to continue taking the paper. Mr. Cannon seemed a little doubtful about our prospects and finally mentioned that it was too bad that Stanley had fallen on his head so violently. Though I had hoped that there might be some simple explanation for all these complex aberrations, I did not dream that the explanation would prove to be so conventional.

"This was in his childhood, Mr. Cannon?" I asked hopefully.

"No. Haven't you heard about Stanley's bicycle accident? Why I thought you had read about it in the paper."

"We have missed a few copies of the paper, you know."

"That's right. Well, Stanley was out riding on his bicycle one day about two weeks ago. He had a friend of his on the fender behind him. As they approached the edge of a good-sized cliff at the local stone quarry, Stanley announced to his formerly trusting friend that he was now planning on riding both of them over the cliff on the bike. The friend, knowing that this was not outside the realm of probability, immediately jumped backwards off the bike, thus shooting Stanley forward over the cliff. Stanley awakened about four hours later in the hospital with a brain surgeon and a neurologist standing over him wondering how serious it might be. They decided after a few days that he should go home and quit his paper route for a few months. Stanley went home but continued his paper route. He hasn't been very regular lately, has he?"

The Sore Toe

One morning as I was making my usual Dagwoodian dash for the front door on my way to work, Mr. Cannon rolled open the huge oak sliding door to his living room with a house-shaking crash and greeted me with a thunderous, "Do you have a minute to spare, Doctor?" Now usually my name was Bill. Consequently, whenever my name became "Doctor," I knew that the time had come for another of those free professional calls.

Mr. Cannon was always very diplomatic in his approach for these curbstone consultations. It was never, "I would like to have you take care of this difficulty." The approach was more often, "I just want you to take a look at something that I have wrong with me and see if you think it's bad enough so that I should see a doctor." This last phrase intimated that he didn't really consider me a physician, at least not in his subconscious. This is always a winning remark to someone who has been licensed to practice medicine for about five years. However, Mr. Cannon was so kindhearted by nature that you could never take offense at remarks of this sort.

"Why sure," I replied, "I still have four minutes before I see my first patient." A clever remark like this was always sure to bring forth gales of ear-splitting laughter. When the commotion had subsided, Mr. Cannon sat down in one of his old rockers and pulled up one opposite him. "It's my toe," he offered in way of explanation. He then pulled off an old battered shoe and a thick black woolen sock.

This procedure exposed a big toe that looked like it had spiked an overripe tomato. It was fiery red, swollen, and hot to the touch. "However did you ever get this?" I asked. "When did you first notice this?"

"Well, sir, I don't exactly know. Guess when I was moving that old lumber over to a new place I did notice a little picking

158

in my shoe. Yes, sir, I noticed that picking for two or three days. Then it got to be a right smart pick. I thought I had better take a look in my shoe and see what was causing all this. Well, sir, you know I found that I had run a nail through my shoe and that it had been sticking into my toe all this time."

Mr. Cannon was all quite matter-of-fact about this. I, of course, immediately pictured him dying with tetanic seizures with the frozen smile on his face of Rizus Sardonicus. However, it was hard to picture Mr. Cannon in a sardonic smile and besides I was now about ten minutes late for my first legal patient. "Yes," I said, "I think that is serious enough for you to see a doctor and get some shots to prevent anything from happening to that toe. In the meantime start soaking it in a pail of hot water or put hot compresses on it. Stay in bed as much as you possibly can, and keep the foot elevated so that you will get good drainage."

That night when I came home from work, Mr. Cannon was faithfully lying on the sofa with his foot swathed in hot wet compresses. It was sticking up into the air like a flag of the crusader for health, which he was at the time. This was not like Mr. Cannon to carry out advice so religiously, and I decided he must be seriously ill. Sure enough, the next morning he started to beat down our door with his loud knock before I was out of bed.

"Good morning, Doctor. I wondered if you could spare a moment." Without further ado, he sat down on the daybed and again pulled off his old shoe and thick wool sock. The toe was not really quite beautiful in the early morning light, from a strictly medical point of view. It differed from its picture of the day before only in that it was a little brighter.

"You know, I soaked this thing yesterday, like you said, and it isn't any better today." He looked at me as though I had really let him down.

I explained to him that it would take some time and a lot of bed rest and strenuous soaking. I could see that he thought this was all quite a hopeless proposition.

"Couldn't you cut it open?" he asked.

It became evident in the next few days that Mr. Cannon was just too busy to spend all his time resting in bed and soaking that little old toe. We saw him making his usual two or three dozen trips a day from his beloved junk-filled basement through his well-worn winding path to his other two houses a couple of doors away. What he did there we never knew. In our minds he more or less walked out that pathway to nonexistence and then clattered right back into his basement again with a slam of the basement door. He also made long trips to the dump with his little rattly red wagon, not to take cans to the dump but to bring back new supplies to store in his basement.

About a week after his last visit with me, all these various important and somewhat mysterious activities began to tell on his toe and so he again brought his toe to see me. This time he became quite insistent on surgery as opposed to just rest and soaking. I suggested that he drop over to the hospital and visit the surgery clinic to get their advice.

That evening Mr. Cannon met me as I came in the house. "Well, sir, I am very well pleased with my visit to the surgeon today. Yes, sir, he gave me some very sound advice, I would say. I think I will get along all right now."

"What did he say? Did he cut it open?"

"No, he suggested that I soak it. He was an older fellow than most of them. Guess he had just returned from the service," he offered in way of explanation for this radical new treatment. "Yes, sir, he seemed to be a pretty smart fellow."

The Era of Our First House: Crumb Cottage— 3171 LaSalle Drive

Mary-Martha lost our first two pregnancies before Andy came along. When she began to take long walks alone in the evening, I decided that it would be cheaper and more effective to buy any kind of a house than to have her go to a psychiatrist. When my salary had increased to $1,200 a year, we found a house that a woman had built with her own hands. Its greatest virtue was that it was located on one acre of land. At last, we did not have to worry about loud noises from neighbors in adjoining apartments!

When Mary-Martha later explained to a friend that our house was only twenty-four by twenty-three feet in size and no two sides were the same length, her friend told her she thought a twenty-three by twenty-four-foot living room was very adequate. Mary-Martha had to explain to her again that it was not the living room that was twenty-four by twenty-three but the entire house!

Mary-Martha's widowed mother was outstandingly generous with her time spent caring for us and our problems. She offered to use any money she had to help us buy that house. I pointed out to my father that the last thing I wanted was to take a widow's money from her because my father was a retired corporation president. He, therefore, gave us $3,400 with a contract stating that we would pay it back at $40 a month, but he did not charge us interest!

The only reason we could move into the house is because, five years after we were married and five and one half years after my M.D. degree, we could buy our first car.

My father pointed out to me that Mr. Mautner and Mr. Krause had left us a small wedding gift, which Dad had invested satisfactorily and was willing to give us now to purchase that car.

A stairway to the upstairs had never been built.

There was no floor upstairs and no sidewalk.

There were no walls inside the two-by-four studs except for two drywall boards put up to sort of outline a kitchen.

There was no insulation and no back porch or front porch.

There was an outhouse. We hired a student to build a septic tank disposal field arrangement so that we could have an inside toilet.

We got a nonregistered plumber to install plumbing for the downstairs bathroom and kitchen. Each day the plumber would show me what he had accomplished and then he would turn on the water and drive away. Immediately I would find leaks in his pipe joints and leave notes for him for the following day.

We had the original electrician for the "kitchen" finish the job for the house. I found that it is common for each worker to start out by severely criticizing the work of "whoever installed" the previous beginning. This time, I was ready for the electrician since I had hired the same electrician who had installed the elementary previous beginning electrical connections and

161

had his paid bill with his name, date and address on it. When he looked at the previous work, he asked me who the dumbbell was who had made such a lousy job of the previous electrical installation. When I showed him his previous paid bill, that ended his discussion.

I worked as a mason to install a front porch and back porch and sixty-two feet of cement sidewalk. Many of my neighbors came over to see what I was doing and were amazed that an *impoverished doctor* could do manual labor so intelligently! Mary-Martha and I both did the drywall and tape, and I painted the drywall with a special textured paint to hide the seams. The house was on an acre of land surrounded by people who worked as attendants at gasoline stations, etc. The only reaction we got from our neighbors as we were making this shack into a house was their concern that the woman who had built the house had installed curtains in all the windows, but we did not even have curtains. They wondered if we were going to get curtains because everyone else on our street had curtains in their windows!

Mary-Martha was pregnant with our second child during this time and, at about five o'clock in the morning the third morning after we moved all of our belongings into "Crumb Cottage" (3171 LaSalle Drive), she awakened me to tell me that she was having contractions. I immediately called my mother in Saginaw to come to take care of Andy while I took Mary-Martha to the hospital for her delivery. (Our second son, Will Beierwaltes, was born that day, October 6, 1947.) Mother came to our new house, took one look inside, and put Andy into her car and drove back to Saginaw. I had to spend an hour getting dressed to go to work in the morning because I did not have the slightest idea where my shorts, ties, socks, shoes and underwear had been dumped in the "new house." After three years of work on this house, we had a new house built for us at 1204 Bydding Road and sold Crumb Cottage for $5,900!

The Era of Our Second House—1204 Bydding Road

Our new house on Bydding Road was in a good neighborhood with everyone about our age and with children the same ages as ours. The house was a one-story ranch *on an acre of land*! It had a garbage disposal, a dishwasher, a laundromat, etc.!! We built a wading pool in back of the kitchen window so that Mary-Martha could keep an eye on the children. We were to have an attic for storage. One day we visited the construction and found that the attic was *filled* with heating ducts for perimeter heating downstairs. Our only storage left was the one-car carport!

Mary-Martha was due to deliver our third child, Marty, on August 27, 1950. We had lived at 3171 LaSalle Drive for three years. Marty came two weeks before we were to move, and 1204 Bydding would not be ready until after Thanksgiving. By this time, I was an assistant professor earning $4,000 a year. Paul Barker, my friend and temporary acting chairman of the Department of Medicine, was very concerned when he found that, for lack of money between houses, we had to move to my parents' cottage at Aplin Beach on Saginaw Bay a hundred miles north of Ann Arbor. The cottage was a frame cottage, heavily mildewed, with front and back porches and no insulation. When I reported to Paul that the first snow there left Mary-Martha with snow inside the cottage, he and his wife, Thelma, asked us to move into his house and occupy the second floor. They would live in a suite in the first floor that they had built for their parents. It was a beautiful house on Vinewood or "Pill Row" (so called because of all the doctors who had residences on that street).

The Era of Our Third House—1885 Fuller

After seven years on Bydding Road, in December 1958, we bought a much bigger house that had been a large part of a mansion located where the present-day Ann Arbor Veterans Administration Hospital stands. It had been moved downhill to 1700 Fuller Road, and the dining room section of the house was installed next to our house. Each of our three bedrooms was huge. The master bedroom was sixteen feet square, but it looked to me like it was twenty-four feet square. Every bedroom

163

had a bathroom and walk-in storage area. The house also had a complete apartment in the basement (kitchen, bathroom, bedroom, and living room). There was also a workroom and room for a Ping-Pong table and pool table. It had a huge screened-in porch overlooking the Huron River, and our lot extended to the river. There was also a double carport but no garage. It was on the edge of the university golf course near the University Hospital.

The only misadventure that I recall during the twelve years we lived at 1885 Fuller Road was that Mary-Martha was found to have pulmonary tuberculosis that she had probably gotten from either me or her sister, Grace, who had had childhood tuberculous lymphadenitis. She had to go to bed at University Hospital for four months.

We got a wonderful woman to keep up the house and care for the kids (until Grandma could come). She was very proud one night when I came home. She had mastered the laundry and ironing machines and had done "seventeen loads" of laundry. The next morning the kids announced that they didn't have any clothes to wear to school! The answer? The cleaning lady, of course, did not know what socks, underwear, etc., belonged to which child, so she just dumped them all in a pile in the upstairs hall.

Our kids walked with me through the golf course across to the railroad tracks, which ran beside the back of the University Hospital. They then walked from University Hospital to the University High School every morning and commonly dropped in to see me on their way home in the evening to see if I was available to walk home with them.

We also played tennis together on the University Hospital tennis courts and the Moser Jordan dormitory tennis courts across the street. I had always taken the kids off Mary-Martha's hands every Saturday afternoon for winter sports in the winter (sledding, skating, and later iceboating and snow skiing) and boating on Barton Pond in the summer. On Sunday afternoons, Mary-Martha joined us to complete the family activities or enlarge upon them.

One Saturday I came home at noon and asked where the kids were. Mary-Martha said they were all out with their friends for the afternoon. I said, "What about me?" She said, "Well, if you are lost and don't know what to do with yourself, there is always me!" So, we went sailing together on Barton Pond to "play together" for the first time in a long time.

Will was now captain of the track team and the football team, and Marty was a cheerleader. All their friends came to our basement every Friday or Saturday. We decided to have the parents of these kids over for a social evening every time the kids had a party. Therefore, no one could ask, "Do your children know where their parents are?" or "Do you know where your children are and what they are doing?" Everyone seemed to have a very good time, young and old.

Larry Hagman

The most exciting thing that happened to us in that house was when a friend of Mary-Martha's called and said, "I know you have a complete apartment in your basement that you never rent out. I also know that your brother, George E. Nichols III, got his master's degree in drama at Yale (before Meryl Streep and Paul Newman) and that you and your husband, Bill, always go to the University of Michigan Drama Festival each spring. I have responsibility to ensure proper housing for the actors and actresses who come to act in this two-week series of plays. We have a young man who insists on bringing his wife and young daughter with him, and he does not want them in a hotel room. His name is Larry Hagman and his mother is Mary Martin. His wife's name is Mai and his three-year-old daughter's name is Heidi."

Mary-Martha felt sorry for them and took them in. They were very social and wonderful people. They were with us for two weeks and we became fast friends. Several well-known movie stars were in Ann Arbor at the same time to act in the plays. Larry and Mai had a cocktail party every evening in our basement. One vivacious actress who had graduated from the University of Michigan and was now on a weekly TV show titled, *Love That Bob; the Bob Cummings Show*. She played the part of Bob's assistant and had the stage name of "Schultze" in

165

that series. Our daughter Marty regularly watched that show, and her eyes bugged when she found "Schultze" in her own basement every night. She would say, "You know the part that I liked in your show last week was when you said to Bob, 'reciting a line verbatim.'" Schultze had to remind Marty that it was nice to be liked but she needed some time with her friends.

When Larry, Mai, and Heidi had to leave, they said, "Let's keep in touch. We have an apartment in New York City. When can you come?" I told them that we had reservations made for Mary-Martha, me, and my father to go to the International Thyroid Meeting in London and our first stop was in New York City to see the museums. They were pleased when we gave them the dates because Mary Martin was the lead in *The Sound of Music* at that time and would be delighted to entertain after her show. We did go, and Mary Martin, Larry Hagman, and his wife were wonderful.

Larry had a very popular TV show after that called *I Dream of Jeannie.* As everyone knows, later he really hit it as the lead in *Dallas* as J.R. This role lasted for years.

When Mary-Martha and I later circled the world in connection with my work, we found that J.R. and *Dallas* were more popular and more well known internationally than anything else in the United States.

The Era of Our Fourth House—1405 Forest Avenue: The Architect's Dream

One day, after fourteen years, Mary-Martha announced to me that we at last had paid off the mortgage on our house at 1885 Fuller Road over a period of twelve years and she asked me whether I wanted to move or stay there the rest of my life. To make a long story short, in 1970 we bought an architect's dream house on 1.9 acres of land, 130 feet above the Barton Pond (a dilation of the Huron River) at 1025 Forest Road for $95,000. We sold our house on Fuller for $34,000. We kept our canoe in front of our new house on Barton Pond and used it almost daily. Barton Hills had a community pool, which was a five-minute drive from our house. The community had fields of corn and asparagus abutting the pool. When we finished a swim, we would pick one ear of corn for each person and asparagus ad lib and, in five minutes, would be home and putting it in boiling water for eating off the cob that evening.

There were numerous woodland walks to take starting right at our house. The family very much enjoyed these walks.

When the kids all left for college, we took up Barton Hills square dancing and ballroom dancing during the winter and cruising in Lake Erie in the summer, about forty minutes away. I have previously described how we got into large sailboat racing and cruising all over the world.

When I retired from the University of Michigan on June 30, 1987, at age seventy-one, we had lived at 1405 Forest Road in Barton Hills for seventeen years. We suddenly found, much to our horror, that our disposal field and septic tank had stopped working because our next-door neighbor above us had made a huge installation above our field. We were told that we should hire a local company of engineers who took care of this type of problem in Barton Hills. They had installed the disposal field and septic tank for the house above us and were sorry but that was not their problem. They also announced that our 1.9 acres of land had no other site with the proper requirements of sand, clay, etc., to allow us to install another septic tank and disposal field.

Thus, our house that we were about to sell for $450,000 was "valueless." I was despondent and decided that, since my salary had been terminated and my retirement annuity had not yet started, I had better seek work. One of my former trainees, Walter Di Giulio, who was chief of the Department of Nuclear Medicine at St. John Hospital in Detroit, Michigan, had just died of a heart attack. Herb Krickstein, M.D., Chairman of the Department of Pathology, and Ed Powsner, M.D., acting head of the Department of Nuclear Medicine, gave me a job as consultant, but they promised to replace me with a younger man in six months. We had such a good time together that I stayed on as one of three senior staff members for seven years.

In the meantime, I had entered the new University Hospital cafeteria despondent about our house and lot. I sat down next to a big stranger who was wearing a white T-shirt and asked him what he did for a living. He said that he did many things. I asked, "Like what?" He said that over the past weekend he had built a new disposal field and septic tank for his father-in-law. I almost screamed as I grabbed his shirt and said, "You did what?!" He was a most unusual man in every way, but he successfully installed new facilities for us that met all the proper criteria.

Every night when I came home, he needed money or raised some excitement. One day, I received an announcement that the liability insurance on our property had just expired. The next day, one of our bulldozers on a huge piece of equipment realized that his machine was about to go over the cliff behind our house with him on it because the brakes did not work. Fortunately, he leaped off just in time before the equipment went over the cliff!

The Era of Our Fifth House—
917 Whittier in Grosse Pointe Park

Mary-Martha and I both became concerned about my daily commute from Ann Arbor to St. John Hospital in Detroit. When passing trucks threw waves of salted slush onto my windshield and my windshield washer fluid reservoir had suddenly gone dry, I found myself staring through a translucent white windshield visualizing vague red taillights flashing on and off some place in front of me.

We therefore sold our house in Ann Arbor, and Mary-Martha bought a smaller house in Grosse Pointe Park, a ten-minute drive from St. John Hospital. Most of this drive was east on Jefferson, with beautiful sunrises and sunsets and racing sailboats on Lake St. Clair.

Although the new house was not the architect's fairyland dream house that we had in Ann Arbor, it was our first house that did have (1) a garage, (2) an automatic lawn sprinkling system, (3) bathrooms that were comfortably warm first thing in the morning set by the clock, (4) air-conditioning, and (5) an audio sentry alarm system.

168

A doctor told me to stop saying I lived in Detroit. I asked him what the main difference was between Grosse Pointe and Detroit. He said that the main difference was that the response time for the alerted police in Grosse Pointe was five minutes and in Detroit it was five and a half hours!

As usual, we joined the nearest Presbyterian church, which was within walking distance of our house on Lake St. Clair and East Jefferson.

Friends asked me to join the Detroit Academy of Medicine. It was there that I ran into my former board job and Phi Chi Medical Fraternity brother and friend, Ed Shumaker. Ed solved "all my financial problems" by inviting his investment counselors in Brundage, Story and Rose to take me on. They achieved a 19 percent increase in our equity in a well-developed portfolio with two investment trusts, one in each of our names.

It was most enjoyable to renew my friendship with Ed Shumaker after having worked board job with him in 1934-35. He was three years ahead of me in school and age.

Through our Presbyterian church's "Let's Brunch" program, we met Barb Braden and she got us together with Phil Dickinson, a retired lawyer, who had worked for AAA most of his life. He had sailed, raced, and cruised and owned his own twenty-two-foot sloop, an Ensign in the Grosse Pointe Park marina.

Mary-Martha and I bought a Beneteau Oceanus 350, a thirty-four-foot-keel cabin cruising sloop from Sun and Sail. We then joined the Detroit Yacht Club where I had swum laps twenty-five minutes a day ever since. We also then took friends sailing with us regularly on Saturdays and Sundays, including Phil and Jean Dickinson and Millie and Lee Danielson from Ann Arbor.

We also began to take tours on ships with my brother Jack and his wife, Ginny. The tour from Rio to Cape Horn was unique in that we rounded Cape Horn twice in a *dead calm* during a formal cocktail party and then went on to Peru. We also went to the Galapagos Islands with the University of Michigan alumni group and made new friends on that trip.

Retirement from Medical Practice, August 30, 1994

I gradually talked my boss, Ed Powsner, into getting rid of my night calls, then weekend calls, then nuclear medicine procedures, and finally I saw thyroid patients only. Finally, on August 30, 1994, at age seventy-seven, I retired permanently from seeing patients and stopped my malpractice insurance.

In the meantime, I had helped Ed Powsner and Dr. Mike Joh replace me with Rick Hay, M.D., Ph.D., from the University of Michigan Nuclear Medicine Division, which I had founded.

Ed budgeted money for me to represent them in tumor conference on Tuesday noon during the lunch hour and be a consultant for him on the topics posed during their past weeks on difficult thyroid patients.

It occurred to Mary-Martha and me that we should now enter into the next phase of our life, namely for me to do something that I enjoy other than medicine.

We purposely, therefore, went to the University of Michigan Retirement Annuitants Association program put on by the Turner Geriatric Clinic in Ann Arbor. We were absolutely delighted to find that this geriatric department and facility may be one of the best in the nation. Ruth Campbell presented the highlights of the services available through the Turner Clinic and stated that it was a very common thing for people in their sixties and seventies to want to write something about their life that they knew the best. This was encouraged, particularly with the excellent help from the university in creative writing. At present, she said that they have five creative writing groups and, with the encouragement and skill available, these people had started to publish commonly.

It occurred to me, that every time that I had told friends about my thrill of the Newport-to-Bermuda race or Charlie Christie, etc., they had encouraged me to publish these stories. I was lucky to find an excellent word processor to help me and I already had a good home dictaphone.

In the meantime, I found that the mayor of Detroit and just about every figure I've heard of is writing his or her memoirs or biography, usually with the help of an expert writer.

Thus, I feel very much at ease and happy about telling what I know best at this age.

As my friend, associate, and temporary acting chairman of the Department of Medicine at the University of Michigan, Paul Barker, once said, "The principal thing wrong with retirement is that there is no future in it."

The main advantage of retirement is that I am no longer committed to a regular, eight-hour, demanding schedule every minute of the day for at least five days a week.

With the discontinuation of patient problems to think about twenty-four hours a day, I have lost my insomnia for the first time in my life. If I am awakened at night by some other problem of mine, I can make a decision right then about what I am going to do about the problem the next day and go back to sleep.

The literature states that the number one killer is heart disease and number three is stroke. Recently, the results of big studies have been published showing that the incidence of heart attacks (? also strokes) is linearly related to pounds over ideal weight. I keep my weight at 134 pounds.

The literature also has proven that twenty-five minutes of continuous exercise sufficient to raise the heart rate above 100 beats per minute definitely decreases the incidence of heart attacks. I love to swim twenty-five minutes a day at the Detroit Yacht Club, and I feel wonderfully euphoric after the swim. Then I come home and play pool with Mary-Martha.

I have warned her that she must *never* precede me in death. She is the only one in this household who knows how to cook and who to call if we need someone regarding the electricity, gas, painting, furnace, garbage disposal, Ameritech, etc. The two of us have also found that, if we get together over the road maps before going to the theater, concert, opera, etc., we can work out a detailed driving strategy and she serves as chief navigator. We can also drive the 250 miles up to Petoskey to see our daughter Marty or drive to Florida for a vacation together because we can alternate naps. By my family statistics, I will precede her in death, thank God!

Soul Mates

As far as the husband-wife relationship is concerned, it is obvious that Mary-Martha and I are soul mates through long and numerous experiences and discussions and have great knowledge and understanding of each other. We also see "eye to eye" on every aspect relating to our children and grandchildren, including eventually transmitting our money to them and helping them increase their quality of life while we are alive.

Most people, during their sixties, experience the loss of pubic and axillary hair, which signifies a loss of testosterone and dehydroepiandrosterone for both sexes. Loss of testosterone signifies a loss of both passion and the willingness to take on uncomfortable sports and their dangers. Indeed, osteoarthritis becomes a way of life. It is disturbing however, to not even be able to put your arm or your body around your spouse in bed without experiencing osteoarthritic pain.

It is also disturbing to realize in one's seventies that, although one's grandchildren are still interesting and beautiful, they also tire you more easily with transmitting to you their endless and needless upper respiratory infection viruses, with their louder and louder noise, and with their endless activity. A great satisfaction, however, at this age is to have the money for the first time in one's life to give judiciously to one's children and grandchildren, particularly to help them solve many of the constant financial problems that could decrease the quality of their lives.

It is hard to stop decorating your home with a Christmas tree and lights when you are going to be off with one of your children's family in another city. You also find that you have to share your kids more and more with other parents-in-law.

It is also difficult to watch your older siblings and their spouses deteriorate and move into "retirement homes."

It is even more difficult to have someone suggest, on the day of retirement, that you should get on a waiting list to move into a retirement home yourself so that you "will be cared for and have lots of friends."

How Much Time Is Left?

Nevertheless, it is important to look at death as an integral part of life. Death means that your chance to do things on this earth have a strict end point. You, therefore, learn to plan your time for your home affairs as carefully as you had planned your time in relationship to your job.

We therefore spent endless hours with a corporation interested in retirement planning, listing our expenditures, assets, and plans to transmit money to our children and grandchildren and avoid federal taxes that would decrease our ability to help our kids do better than we did to advance civilization.

We also spend more time cultivating our friendships with contemporaries who are active through the church, pot-luck clubs, the Detroit Yacht Club, etc. It is also fun to see the world's objective recognition of your "contributions to civilization" as listed in the chapter "Medicine," in *The World's Who's Who in Science from Antiquity to the Present*, *Who's Who in the World*, *The Best Doctors in America*, and the highest award for the greatest scientific achievement of any doctor in the United States.

Mary-Martha Enabled My Career

My wife has been with me at every such recognition and heard me state with emotion that I would never have been able to accomplish any of these without her constant support and guarding of my time.

I am also deeply indebted to her understanding and thoughtful care to release me from family obligations of caring for the children when I had a chance to race in the Port Huron-to-Mackinaw and Chicago-to-Mackinaw races and the Newport-to-Bermuda race, etc. Indeed, one of the joys that we have at this age since I retired is to be able to be together in the same house sharing daily experiences on everything, but, at the same time, making certain that the other partner is completely free to do whatever she/he wants to do whenever she/he wants to do it.

Since I am home, I now make certain that I do the dishes daily while she does the cooking. The two of us also make certain together that the trash and the recycling material is ready at the curbstone every Tuesday night after five o'clock for pickup the next morning. At this time, the tasks of daily living in our own house, independent of our children and grandchildren, or in a retirement "community," are much more appealing than living in a one-bedroom apartment in a retirement home.

Our Children

Why Have Children?

In retrospect, the one thing that God makes certain of and that almost everyone assists Him/Her in is in reproducing the human race. I believe that this is due to our genes that produce hormones that have been present for millions of generations because we are "the survivors."

I remember almost the day when Mary-Martha got "the hots" to have her first pregnancy. I saw it again when our favorite daughter-in-law (our only daughter-in-law), Patricia, got "the hots" to have her first child. Similarly, it must be genes that convince a woman that she should go on to have a second or third child. (Of course, I have also had a lot of indigent patients who were pregnant again and again and again every time I saw them. They told me that there was no rationale for this. It was just that they couldn't seem to stop getting pregnant.)

One very attractive and intelligent patient, the wife of a professor of neurology at the University of Michigan, whom I had treated for thyroid cancer with a total thyroidectomy and radioactive iodine, wanted a third child immediately. She had graduated with honors from Radcliffe. When I asked her why she wanted a third child immediately, even before I had finished treating her cancer, she replied, "Because all my friends on our street are having a third child!"

Should Children Get Straight As?

Mary-Martha and I were certain that our parents, though subtly put, had trained us to be superachievers with a powerful weapon of "the higher the grades, the more the praise." With some parents, the idea is fairly definitely stated, "I will love you if you get straight As and I won't if you don't." One successful engineer, with whom I shared a rental car from an airport, told me that all three of his children all had straight As. When I told him that this was an exceptional achievement and asked him if he had any explanation for this, he replied that he knew exactly why they did. He had told them, in no uncertain terms, that, if they ever got anything less than an A, he would not speak to them again until they brought home an A in that same course. He had stuck to his promise and he pointed out that it had a devastating effect on the child and they kept clear in their mind that they must get straight As.

Our daughter, Martha, and her husband, Pat, had made it clear that all three of their children were going to Notre Dame and they would need all As to get in. They have both contributed immensely to helping their children with their homework. Marty and Pat are well aware of many children under such circumstances who "escaped" home to go to college and then promptly flunked out of college. Marty has elected to continue the daily pressure watchfully. I believe she is probably right because we never put pressure on our children to get straight As, and I realize that the only excuse for Cs and Ds was lack of parental pressure. I now realize that children learn from daily repetitive little sermons and lectures from their parents. If a parent says to his or her child, "I am only going to say this once," they will rarely respond.

The Exceptional Child

Mary-Martha and I agreed in advance of her first pregnancy that we would pray for having normal average children because of the tremendous stress that can be put upon a parent who has an "exceptional" child. It was only later that I learned that every human being's genes are different from every other human being's. An excellent research obstetrician at the University of Michigan taught me that the vagina, cervix, and uterus select the proper sperm from others to acquire different genes than those of the mother's egg. Most remarkably, there is apparently solid evidence that this selection is done at the time of the next impregnation to be certain that the genes in the second child are different from those in the first child. There is evidence, but not proof, that this happens a third time to differentiate the third child from both the first and the second.

Andy

Needless to say, our first child was exceptional beyond description. It was forty-five years later that the description of dyslexia became known to doctors and parents. Mary-Martha lost her first two pregnancies during the first trimester, even though she had been at complete bed rest for unexplained spotting. When Andy came we had the services of possibly the best professor of obstetrics at the University of Michigan. When he walked into the delivery room, Andy's legs were hanging down outside of Mary-Martha (frank breech). The umbilical cord was also hanging down (prolapsed cord) with the danger of a compressed umbilical artery, which would cause hypoxia in the child. When the obstetrician started to deliver Andy, he found Andy's right arm was caught underneath the back of his head (nuchal arm) and he had to cut open the cervix and uterus (Dührsen's incision) in order to deliver him. Each of these complications occurring separately in previous cases had been fatal to a child!

The first symptom that Andy was not normal was that he required a full-length bib for his constant drooling. The second symptom was that he was actually brilliant in acquisition and retention of new knowledge but could not tie his shoes while expounding accurately on the quantitative structure of the solar system. Also, he ate with his fingers long after his contemporaries had learned to eat with silverware, etc.

No doctor had an explanation. We had his hearing and vision checked, and they were perfect. His IQ registered over 200 repeatedly in most areas, but there some unexplained serious dips in his IQ in certain areas. We then hired the best professor of child psychiatry to diagnose and treat him. When we realized that one of Andy's greatest failings was that he was disorganized, we also hired an older expert teacher to be his "secretary." She found he would take a written test in school and then unwittingly put it in his pocket and take it home without turning it in for a grade. He would do his written homework but forget to take it to school, etc. These explanations were helpful to the teacher who announced to us in a PTA meeting that she had no record of completion of any written assignments by Andy for the entire semester. She wanted to know what we planned to do about it.

I remember the day, the hour, and the location that I finished teaching Andy to read when he was in the fifth grade. As usual, we were in the car waiting for Mary-Martha and I was having him read to me as I did in every spare minute. The most exceptional thing to me was his absolutely encyclopedic knowledge of just about everything without ever being able to read until he was well into the fifth grade.

One time his geography teacher (also his homeroom teacher) at the University High School in Ann Arbor complained that Andy did not like his maps of Europe plastered around the entire inside of his classroom. The teacher said that the maps actually upset Andy considerably, and he suggested that we get help for Andy. Since the maps were of the changing geography of Europe during successive wars, I asked the number one professor of history at the University of Michigan, Preston Slosson, to join us as we looked at the maps with Andy to help find a solution for his problem. He was delighted to do so, perhaps in part because his daughter had been a patient of mine. When Slosson entered the room and read the name of the map maker, he whispered to me that that series of maps was the most historically inaccurate of all maps available. He then asked Andy what bothered him about the maps. In response to questioning, Andy showed Slosson on the map the incorrect dates and geography for a given time period. Slosson agreed completely and found Andy deadly accurate on each point. Andy confirmed that the maps' inaccuracy was very upsetting to him.

When the teacher we had hired to help Andy went with him to the classroom, she found that he sat at the back end of the classroom and was highly distracted by all the activity of his colleagues in front of him. When that teacher had Andy switched to the front of the room, he was able to concentrate more fully on the subject matter and achieved better.

In his daily assignments in mathematics at University High, Andy found that the students in his class would be given several routine mathematical problems, then a more difficult problem, and then a problem that no one was really expected to be able to solve. Of course, Andy immediately began to work on the "impossible" problems. He solved all of them. His teacher would not infrequently call in other teachers to talk with Andy about his methods of solving the problems. They were astounded that he rarely used the one or two methods accepted for solving these problems but had originated his own methods of solving the "impossible" problems correctly.

When Andy tried to read or spell, we found a specific sign common to most people with dyslexia, that is, the inability to differentiate "ON" from "NO!" He also read upside down and backwards by preference! Thirty-five to forty years later, these were found to be classical signs of dyslexia.

We also later found out that many children with dyslexia eventually become highly successful. In every instance that I have probed, I found that at least one parent never gave up the belief that the child was educable. One dyslexic radiology and nuclear medicine resident of mine, with almost straight-A average late in medical school, introduced me to his father who told me about the same tale that I could tell him about having a dyslexic son. His son had been declared uneducable by almost everyone, but his father refused to believe these statements. He repeatedly had his son seen by child psychiatrists, tested for vision and hearing, and seen by neurologists. He also spent thousands of hours at home and in his son's classes to learn what he could do to help him.

The experience of finding out that nothing we did with our first baby would cure his troubles and no one knew why he was that way shattered our self-confidence that we were capable of being successful parents.

Furthermore, the child psychiatrist told me that I should spend every possible minute (even at the expense of time with my second and third children) teaching Andy everything in manual dexterity so that he would not be further isolated from his friends and peers. It took me five years to teach Andy how to ride a bicycle and also how to drive a car. The explanation

181

became apparent to me that, if one cannot tell the difference between "ON" and "NO," one could not turn the bicycle handles toward the left to stop the bike from falling to the left, etc. Our Nobel Prize was helping Andy become a successful landscape architect. We took great pride in his graduation from University High School and in his graduation from the University of Michigan School of Landscape Architecture and Design. I later found that, of all his courses in the University of Michigan School of Landscape Architecture and Design, he had completed twenty-three courses in architecture with a composite A-minus average.

Should Kids Work?

All of our kids learned to work while they were being "raised." They were paid an allowance each week at a certain amount for each household task they accomplished. Eventually, this rose to one dollar for washing and cleaning the car once a week. They were also paid one dollar for cleaning out and resetting the fireplace with logs. Other parents told me that they did not believe in paying kids for doing these household chores because they were all members of the same family and should do those chores as part of the family team. I would then ask them if their children routinely and weekly did the numerous tasks we had laid out for our children and they said no. I said, "That's why I pay them."

It is of interest to me that our kids were most fascinated by the concept of "unearned income," namely the interest that compounded in their individual credit union accounts. Later, they were expected to get a well-paying summer job each year that had to be secured the previous December. I told them that, if they failed to get a job by December, I would get a job for them in January. That furnished plenty of motivation for them to go out and get their own jobs.

Unfortunately for Andy, a recession in construction occurred while he was in college. He was at Kalamazoo College in 1963 and graduated from the University of Michigan in January 1971. He did get summer jobs, however, and they contributed knowledge that he could not have received otherwise.

This long history of good job experience is very important in his curriculum vitae. His first full-time job with a corporation was with Commonwealth Associates. They published a beautiful curriculum vitae of Andy along with his picture in a booklet of advertisement that they used to attract others to their corporation. One of his jobs in Tennessee was to decide where high-voltage electrical transmission should be laid out in a town. His employers suddenly found that he was an encyclopedia of history and historical details on old houses and buildings. Although he did most of the work on the ground, they also took him up in helicopters to cover the possible path of a power line, and he located and made drawn diagrams of the buildings that should not be disturbed. With the energy crunch, Commonwealth got rid of all 124 landscape architects.

Andy then joined Johnson and Roy in their company, Applied Environmental Issues. They had been professors of his and he liked both them and their company. Suddenly, he found that the University of Michigan had attracted John Johnson away from their company when they made him the dean of the School of Natural Resources, including landscape architecture. It was very difficult for Andy to lose two good jobs in just a few years after his excellent start.

After a big family powwow, we decided that he should go into private practice in landscape architecture in Ann Arbor with his own truck. Fortunately, although not lucrative, he has been very happy with his work and his customers are all intelligent people who love him and appreciate his unique talents as a landscape architect. His customers are particularly intrigued by his encyclopedic and deadly accurate knowledge of the scientific names of all the trees, grasses, weeds, flowers, etc. Most of them have found that, when Andy first walks over their property with them, he discovers some delightful surprise on their property in the form of a historical tree or unique bush with properties that can easily be developed by pruning the surrounding area. He also expanded his snowblowing winters to helping older people in particular with maintenance problems on their property. From early spring to late fall, he has all he can do.

In retrospect, in the process of spending thousands of hours with him since birth, reading to him endlessly and teaching him how to swim, ice skate, ice boat, throw a ball, bat a ball, sail, cruise and race a boat, Andy and I have become intimate and knowledgeable soul mates. Mary-Martha and I take great pleasure in knowing what we gave him in order to aid his own successful efforts as a talented and loving adult. We remember that, from time to time, we were both overwhelmed by the magnitude and complexity of the task and almost total lack of help from well-meaning professionals and unending problems without logical solutions. Only recently have we been able to discuss this easily with others because Andy and we all agree that he had a clear-cut diagnosis of dyslexia. Whenever we became discouraged, it was very helpful to remind ourselves that he was constantly improving over time.

Will

Since the day he was born, Will has always been a joy to behold and be with. He was normal and average in every respect but developed most unusual talents and successes with time, right up to the present writing.

Athletics: Will's body looked like that of a professional athlete with a very high percent of his body composed of muscle mass. I encouraged him to become proficient in sports as we had with Andy and Marty. We gave each of our children private lessons, both by us and by paid professionals, in swimming, tennis, golf, sailing, etc. Our goal was not that they become superstars but rather that they would feel at ease in accepting requests from friends to join them in athletic pursuits.

The first time I saw Will run competitively in track at University High School, I felt sorry for him because his arms and legs were moving fairly aimlessly. I was most impressed to see the results of excellent coaching from his math teacher and coach, Charles Belknap, at his school. Will became captain of the track team, and among other things, he ran on an 880 relay team that won the state championship and set a state of Michigan record for their class. Will looked like a professional in that race. We all rejoiced.

Socializing: Will also became captain of the football team at University High and played on the basketball team. He continued to play football in college. He obviously loved all these sports and became incredibly knowledgeable. From that time until the present, he has continued to keep up with everything that goes on with these sports. He played on a championship soccer team while in the army, and now is deriving great joy from coaching his sons' local soccer teams.

I have related before how we invited all the parents of our children's teammates to party with us in our house on Fuller Road while the kids partied in the basement with a full apartment, pool table, and Ping-Pong table. Will and several of his strong friends served as bouncers if any of the kids coming to the party wanted to drink alcoholic beverages. Those were some of the most wonderful, happy years of our life.

Art and Photography: All three of our kids became skilled artists. It was not by chance.

I have related earlier that, as a child in New Haven, Connecticut, Mary-Martha had private lessons every Saturday morning with the encouragement of her father and the help of a woman who had achieved a master's degree in the Yale School of Art. When Mary-Martha was to start at the Yale School of Art, she skipped the first year by showing the proper people her portfolio that covered everything and more that was taught in the first year at Yale School of Art. She then received a scholarship for the next two years because of her excellence in achievement.

Whenever it rained or life became unusually monotonous at any stage of the development of our three children, Mary-Martha would get out the appropriate art equipment for the age and mood of the child. All three, in my opinion, have produced beautiful works of art. Will, however, was more adventurous than the other two, and was successful in competing in art.

My brother Jack had become an excellent photographer and was in the Sheridan Shores (Chicago Gold Coast) Photography Club. He taught Will a great deal about the technical aspects of good photography. Jack was easily able to have photographs published in the Sunday supplement section of Sunday newspapers.

185

Two of Will's remarkable achievements will serve to illustrate my point:

Art: The U.S. Army announced an "all-army" art competition in various categories while Will was serving at Fort Riley, Kansas (as a 1-AO; conscientious objector who does not object to serving, just killing) during the Vietnam era. Will called Mary-Martha and asked her to send a large and somewhat abstract painting of two Texas long-horned steers he called "Moonstruck Texas Lovers," which he had painted while waiting to enter the army some months earlier. Mary-Martha told him over the phone that she agreed that this was perhaps his best, but the framing did not complement the colors in the painting. She still remembered a poor grade and criticism from one of her professors in art school because she had failed to match her framing in such a fashion. Will finally agreed to change the framing. Mary-Martha packed the painting to be mailed by wrapping it with another painting of his that she disliked, and wanted him to get rid of. He entered both paintings plus several watercolors he had recently done and a couple of pencil sketches. In the first round in the Midwest region, the large paintings won first and second place, and he also placed first and third in watercolor and first, second, and third in drawing. In the next round, including entries from all U.S.-based army personnel, he won first in oil/acrylic for the "Lovers" and first in drawing. In the final round, including entries from all U.S. and foreign-based army personnel, the "Lovers" won a "Purchase Award" from a museum, which we understand is in Fort Sill, Oklahoma.

Photography: When Will went to the Mayo Clinic to start his post-doctoral fellowship in hypertension research, he saw a posted announcement for a photography competition. The deadline for submitting entries was that evening, and there were numerous categories with various specific criteria given for judging each photograph in each category. Will submitted three photographs in three categories. He won a first, second, and third place prize with one photograph in each of three categories. I asked him which of his photographs won first place. It was a photograph that he had taken years earlier at Ann

Arbor's Blues Festival, a sort of "Woodstock" held near the University of Michigan North Campus, near our house on Fuller Road. It was a picture of a long-haired male hippie with beard, mustache, etc., with a very young girl sitting on her "father's" shoulders with her legs around his neck facing forward.

Indeed, Will entered many such contests of various sorts, and frequently won.

Mary-Martha also developed our attic on Fuller Road to be a miniature city for the kids, with an electric train, lead toy soldiers, etc. Perhaps because of this background, when he was grown, Will became a dedicated collector of antique lead toy soldiers with a large and eclectic collection. Over time he has acquainted me with some outstanding television sports commentators, actors, and successful businessmen, etc., who share his interest in this hobby. Will has made his own figures and dioramas, and became a consulting editor of a collectors' journal, specializing in toy soldiers, and he even consulted for Christie's antique auction house of New York when they cataloged a collection in Michigan. He has published over thirty articles in the popular press on this subject and has also contributed to a number of books.

Although very obviously bright and well educated, Will never worked very hard at college. After leaving the army, when he went to the University of North Carolina at Chapel Hill to work on his Ph.D. degree in renal physiology, he realized that he had to get very high grades, and he did. While he was in school at Kalamazoo College, I encouraged him to get a job during his summers in the Department of Pharmacology at the University of Michigan. There he became an expert in performing necessary, complex operations and data collection on a variety of research animal models used in experiments. For the first time, he knew that he had achieved something of great satisfaction for himself in science. These experiences were of great importance to the people running the doctoral program at Chapel Hill. One of his teachers at Chapel Hill encouraged him to take a postdoctoral scholarship at the Mayo Clinic in hypertension research. His mentor there, Prof. Carlos Romero, helped place him on the staff of the Hypertension Research Division at

Henry Ford Hospital in Detroit. Mary-Martha and I have been proud of his originality and productivity with numerous scientific publications in his chosen area of research. He became an "Established Investigator" of the American Heart Association, and recently was awarded an associate professorship in the Department of Internal Medicine at Case Western Reserve University School of Medicine in Cleveland, Ohio, with his base laboratory and colleagues at Henry Ford Hospital in Detroit.

Since our move to Grosse Pointe Park after my joining the staffs of St. John Hospital and William Beaumont Hospital, we have found it mutually beneficial to live within a mile of Will's home, also in Grosse Pointe Park. We have particularly enjoyed having him bring his three children over every Tuesday evening for dinner. His wife, Patricia, is a nurse clinician in pediatric neurology with Mike Nigro at Children's Hospital, and she works a clinic or parent support groups on Tuesday evenings there. It has given us the wonderful opportunity to observe the changes that occur in very young developing children from week to week. It is exciting to see these remarkable developments that occur so quickly and so frequently, especially in our own progeny.

On a final note, it also is of interest to me that Will and Patricia fell in love with each other at "first sight" when they met at the Mayo Clinic, just as Mary-Martha and I had fallen in love at "first sight" over fifty years ago.

Martha

I never wanted to press Mary-Martha for another pregnancy to have a daughter because of the tough time she had with pregnancies. However, one day at a fair in Ypsilanti, Michigan, I saw a nice young father walking with his beautiful young daughter. I prayed that Mary-Martha would notice and comment. Much to my surprise, she said that child had made her long to try again for a daughter. She did.

At that time, I believed that there were only cultural differences between very young boys and girls. At a very early age, Marty changed my views on this subject totally.

188

As Marty grew, I read to her every evening in Grandfather's rocking chair and sang her to sleep with lullabies.

At Fuller Road, I made a general point of having a candle-light dinner every evening at 6:00 P.M. with the emphasis that occasion was for each person to tell us what was of interest that day in his or her life. I would then close dinner by asking if anyone had homework, book reports, etc., that needed our help. After the dishes were put away, Mary-Martha used our second-floor landing for sewing, etc. Our bedrooms surrounded this landing. I remember Marty coming to me at 11:00 P.M. one night to tell me that she had forgotten that she had a book report due "tomorrow morning at eight o'clock" on a book she had not yet read. My job was to skim the book with her and lay out the report outline by 1:00 A.M. for her to have ready at 8:00 A.M. I won't discuss the details of how we achieved all this in two hours. I also tried to have a talk with Marty at her bedtime each night so that she could tell me about problems she was not eager to bring up.

Marty was amazingly like me in her degree of being an extrovert and with her love of having lots of friends around. She became the best sailor and swimmer in the family and was on an excellent swim team that won. She was an average student until we brought Ulle Miebs to join us one year on a student exchange from East Friesland when Marty was in the tenth grade. Ulle's father was a teacher, and her two intelligent parents ran a school. Ulle was such a compulsive German when she joined us that she immediately became the least popular girl at University High School. We all liked her and worked with her to change her image. She did so beautifully that she was perhaps the most popular girl at University High School when she left. In the process, Marty learned from Ulle how to study to achieve *A* grades.

Martha's Motivation

Marty had no idea what she wanted to study as a college student training for a career. She enrolled in teaching for the lack of anything better and because she was such a good babysitter. Marty graduated in teaching and immediately decided not to teach. One time, when I invited her to have lunch with me, I asked her if she knew the family's ground rules for such an occasion. She said, "Yes, I have already got a job as an insurance clerk at Bronson Hospital." She asked, "Pop, what is life all about? I don't know what I should be doing in life."

I said, "The most rewarding experiences in life are giving of your skilled services for the benefit of your fellow human beings."

She said, "Like what?"

I said, "Well, you have probably noticed that I am a physician and thoroughly enjoy my work, healing the sick, teaching others how to heal the sick, and doing medical research to help others help patients that I probably will never see."

She said it would be impossible for her to become a doctor. I reminded her that we had talked about this problem before, and she had told me that the reason she could not become a nurse was that she knew she would faint when she saw her first drop of blood. I told her that I could not accept this excuse any more because Bob Buxton, one of my best surgical friends and professor at the University of Michigan Hospital, had told me that he fainted the first time he ever saw a drop of blood. He never fainted again throughout all his medical school and surgical training.

She talked this over later with her brother Will in Kalamazoo. She decided to apply to nursing schools. They told her that her grades were all right but she had never taken any science or mathematics courses. These were requirements to enter all the nursing schools. Therefore, she arranged with Michigan State University in East Lansing, Michigan. At the registration office, they asked her if she wanted to take Zoology 101 or Botany 101 for her first course in science. She said that she wanted to take that course in Human Anatomy. They told her that course was for medical students and had lots of prerequisites that she did not have. She finally talked them into allowing her to take this class because it was at her risk. She took the course, had three major examinations, and achieved a straight-A average in the course.

When they asked her at registration about her second science course, she said she wanted to take the course in Human Genetics. They pointed out to her that there were many prerequisites that she did not have, but they finally allowed her to take it.

One of the first excursions in the course was to a nearby state institution where each student interviewed a patient with a genetic disease. She called me and told me how excited she was to interview an adult subject with Down's syndrome and found out the tremendous changes that genetic disease had caused in his life.

The only nursing school that accepted her was the best—Case Western Reserve in Cleveland, Ohio. Marty and the representative from Case Western sent to interview her really hit it off together (as usual). She told Marty that, if she ever had trouble in nursing school and came to her for a consultation, she would label her as purely "lazy" because anyone who could work off all their science and mathematic requirements in one year (nineteen hours) at Michigan State with an A-minus average could handle any intellectual challenge presented to her in the Case Western Reserve School of Nursing.

The two-year course was for people who had already graduated from college and wanted to get R.N. and B.S.N. degrees. Of course, many of her classmates had graduated from the best women's schools in the East and were obviously very bright and very good students. This was the first real competition that she had struggled against. Almost as important was that her colleagues offered generous criticism of her boyfriends in a constructive manner.

When Marty met the man who was to later become her husband, Patrick Michael Maloney, she consulted me. She said, "Pop, you reminded me in the past that most of my dates were 'creeps.' Now most of my dates are good guys in every respect and the number is constantly increasing. Why do you think that is?"

I said I knew exactly the explanation for this phenomenon. I had never seen anyone mature so rapidly in two years as Marty had in Case Western Reserve School of Nursing with high-class, intelligent associates from good homes, generally speaking. I explained to her that intelligent, attractive, mature young women were recognized by similar young men. I complimented her on her wonderful metamorphosis.

Mary-Martha and I were especially pleased that she favored Patrick because he was a father-in-law's dream. For reasons not presented here, at that time in his life, he wanted most in life to become a good husband and second a good father. He had no debts and had set aside, through his own ingenuity, $6,000 as a down payment toward his first house. He also collected dishes in Ireland. He was handsome and bright and obviously loved Martha. As I have explained to an endless number of people, any father-in-law who could criticize such a son-in-law obviously would be in need of psychiatric help.

We are delighted that Pat works as a cardiologist in the Burns Clinic in Petroskey where they have lots of snow in the winter for skiing and are ideally situated on Little Traverse Bay for boating and swimming in the summer. In addition, they have two cottages on Douglas Lake.

Mary-Martha's father was chairman of the botany department at Yale. The University of Michigan talked him into bringing his wife, three daughters, and son to Douglas Lake every summer to teach at the University of Michigan biological station. All expenses were paid by the university for the entire family. Mary-Martha fell in love with this place and encouraged Marty to get a job there one summer while she was in school at Kalamazoo. She loved it and its Nichols' Laboratory, Nichols' Bog, etc. Pat, Marty, and their three children as well as Mary-Martha and I all love Douglas Lake and spend some vacation time together there every year.

Marty has become a full-time mother, like her mother, and has her kids signed up to develop athletic skills and to achieve A averages. Her children, at early ages, have become outstandingly successful in all their age-appropriate endeavors.

Family Trips before College

The summer before Andy started the twelfth grade, I decided that it was time for the family to take the ultimate camping trip. I had engagements to speak in Chicago and several places in the West and Southwest and planned to attend the national meeting of the Society of Nuclear Medicine. Stringing all these together plus my vacation time allowed me to take a six-week, six-thousand-mile camping trip. We had a new air-conditioned car and bought a camping trailer. I had taught each of the kids how to camp while bow-and-arrow deer hunting. They were skilled at navigating woods with compasses alone. We saw the Grand Canyon, Yellowstone National Park, Mount Rushmore, the Great Salt Lake, Los Angeles, San Francisco, Catalina Island (with my Uncle Bill on his boat), and most of the national parks along the way. Certainly Disneyland was one of the most outstanding visits that we made.

We even had a bear pawing through our luggage at Yellowstone National Park. The boys and I would set up the camping trailer, get out the cooking equipment for Mary-Martha and Marty, and get everything ready for the evening. When the park rangers came to visit us, we would be drinking lemonade and would always offer them a glass of lemonade.

During the trip, when we felt that we had camped enough and were feeling dirty and needed to do laundry and ironing, we would stop in a hotel where we could take care of these things. One of our stops was at a leading hotel in Las Vegas where a famous actor in a very famous film was at the pool mingling with the guests and actually touched Marty. She was overwhelmed by the thought that such a famous actor had touched her. While staying at the hotels, we would go to a dinner theater, swim in the pool during the day, do the laundry. etc.

At the end of the trip, I told Mary-Martha I thought everyone had a wonderful time and asked for her viewpoint. She said that she felt she had done a lot of work on the trip. When I found that Mary-Martha was not entirely pleased with the trip, I proposed that we go cruising in a twenty-eight-foot cruising sailboat out of Charlevoix to the North Channel in Canada, frequently referred to as one of the most beautiful cruising grounds in the world. I reminded her that the boat would have five bunks on it for five people and each person would take care of his or her own bunk. I would be delighted to do the cooking and there would be no taking down and putting up every day since we would be on the boat for three weeks.

It was a delightful trip and we found that each child became totally proficient in cruising a keel sailboat during the first week of that sailing experience. As far as they were concerned, the wind was never strong enough and the waves were never large enough to disturb them.

I reminded the family that these two trips in two years would probably conclude the time when all five of us could get together for extended vacations of this type. All of us have an infinite number of happy memories of those two trips.

The Eternal Search

"Security" of Publications

At seventy-eight years of age, I am positive of only one answer to the most important questions in life: WHY AM I HERE? WHAT SHOULD I DO? WHY?

It is now apparent to me (and has been to others) that the final attainment of a goal is usually less exciting and helpful to an individual than the actual quest.

I remember that at an early age I decided that some day when I retired or faced death I wanted to see clearly and concretely what I had done in life to contribute to the progress of civilization rather than to see my life as a noncontributory series of functions—to be born, perform bodily functions, grow, work for a living, reproduce the human race, and die.

I was required by the University of Michigan to keep a curriculum vitae. It pleased me yearly to assemble my publications, according to year, into nine bound volumes! I also collected records of awards, etc., in newspapers, etc., in my photograph albums.

Reordering Priorities Daily

It has interested me that these have been a great source of satisfaction to me as these recognitions occurred. Since retiring, however, I have rarely looked at any of these visible recognitions of achievement.

This is fortunate because you can continue to evolve spiritually until you die. Indeed, death is most important because it is inevitable and reminds you of how much time you have left. Therefore, at the beginning (or end) of each day, it is helpful to spend some quiet time carefully reordering your priorities in an attempt to achieve your goals.

In 1950, while I was making ward rounds at the Peter Bent Brigham Hospital of Harvard University with George Thorn, M.D., the outstanding chairman of the Department of Internal Medicine, he introduced me to his three-by-five-inch-card method of reordering priorities daily. As he reached into his shirt pocket on the left to pull out a pen and a three-by-five-inch card, he asked me if I used his system of planning. He wrote on a card what should be done each day. He said that at the end of the day he crossed off those chores he had accomplished and then rewrote on a new card what remained undone from yesterday and what should be done the next day. This forces you to reorder your priorities daily. I had never heard of it and immediately (and permanently) adopted his excellent mode of trying to accomplish what efforts one is making to achieve old and new goals.

Spiritual Evolution

The total person is what we call the soul. We love someone as they are rather than because of their build, their genes, their acquired money or social position, their job accomplishments, etc. Thus, our commitment to our fellow souls requires our effort and is helped by small miracles called "grace." A person can continue to enjoy this great pleasure of giving to others progressively until he dies of old age, regardless of decreasing physical strength, hearing, eyesight, etc.

Gifts to Aid Spiritual Evolution

Now that I have reviewed some of the keystones necessary to achieve spiritual evolution, I would like to review what gifts I have been given to help me in this lifelong task.

Genes

Genes. It helped to have no known inherited diseases, such as diabetes, etc., to shorten my lifespan or detract from my progress along this lifelong trail.

Parents

As outlined previously, my parents were gregarious and fun loving. They belonged to the Saginaw Canoe Club before my brother and I were born. Four couples bought a houseboat to socialize on the Saginaw River in Saginaw. When they all had children, my parents first rented a cottage on the beach in

Sebawaing and then bought a cottage on Killarney Beach on Saginaw Bay (off the southwestern corner of Lake Huron).

When my brother Jack and I became teenagers and wanted to dance and see floor shows and visit amusement parks, they bought a cottage on Aplin Beach where there was more protection for our boats, sidewalks to walk on, grass, trees, and a short walk to the amusement park with dance halls, etc., at Winona Beach.

My father drove to the cottage every night to be with us for a long swim, dinner and socializing in the evening after supper. He took me fishing in our outboard (on a rowboat) every Sunday morning that we didn't go to church. We knew where the perch were biting. It was not uncommon to pull up two perch on two hooks on one pole and simultaneously two perch on two hooks on another pole. We kept our fish on a leader in the water so that they were alive until thirty minutes before we ate them. My father and I competed in speed for both cleaning the fish and scaling them. We got our worms out of the ground, using steel rods with wooden handles with black insulated wires. These were hooked onto wires leading from the back of our cottage to the garage behind the cottage. The worms fairly leaped out of the ground when exposed to this electrical field. Dad and I had lots of short and long talks together during the fishing. He was always very careful about what he said and how he said it to his son.

He encouraged us to bring our dates to stay at the cottage over the weekend and go sailing, fishing, dancing, or to the floor shows at the amusement parks, etc.

I have also explained how he instructed me on little jobs to be done each day of the week when he went to work when I was a child. Later he encouraged me to take over my brother's magazine routes. Later my brother and I worked in his clothing store in our spare time. Of course, he was eager for us to take time off to race in sailboat regattas, etc.

Later I was encouraged to work as a nature study counselor instead of at the Chevrolet foundry (where the pay was higher but the danger was greater).

When we were in college, he used to quiz me every time I came home for a visit or they visited me. He asked me what

200

courses I had, what the professors were like, how I liked the professors, what I was learning, how much I was enjoying it, and, lastly, how my grades were. For example, in my sophomore year in undergraduate school at the University of Michigan, I told him I liked physiological psychology but that the professor was an "old man" who carried a skull into his lecture each day with no particular purpose in mind. Dad asked if there was a younger and better man also teaching the same course. I told him there was a younger, outstanding teacher of that course. He persuaded me to request a change to this younger man. I did. I fell in love with the course and got an *A* in it.

The course taught such things as quantitative studies on the learning curve before taking an examination of a course, memory loss after the examination, how many times it was optimal to review material to be memorized before the exam (daily for the last three days before the exam), etc. This knowledge, of course, helped the efficiency of all my future studies.

One Saturday I came home to Saginaw from the university to have a date with my current girlfriend. One of us, probably me, had the wrong date on our calendar, so I had no date on Saturday night. I was depressed and told my parents that I was taking all my studying to the Saginaw Public Library to study that evening. They were deeply concerned and sorry about the "bummer." I always remember how, later that evening, my mother and father came to visit me at the library at about 9:30 to sympathize with me and encourage me to stop studying and come home to be with them. When Jack and I both went off to college, my mother had to have a young high school teacher come rent a bedroom in her house so that they would have a "daughter" around the house to take our place.

Mother was always identifying and aiding poor female children who needed work and pay and other support.

Church

My parents were "always" members of the Warren Avenue Presbyterian church in Saginaw. My brother and I started at Sunday church school at the youngest possible age and were later encouraged to attend church with our parents. My primary interest in the church service at that stage was to look at my girlfriend, Phyllis Sterling, in the choir while she sang. I also tried hard to find something helpful in the sermons of the minister but got very little out of the sermons that I recall.

The church also sponsored a Boy Scout troop, which, of course, my parents had us join. The most difficult thing about Boy Scouts to me was that I had to wear my brother's outmoded Boy Scout uniform and he was eight inches taller than I.

Play Habits

My parents also made certain that during the long winter months I had an active program at the YMCA in swimming and working to become a junior lifesaver and senior lifesaver, etc. It was there that I met Bill Moon from Arthur Hill High School. He, representing Arthur Hill, and I, representing Saginaw Eastern, each started the competitive swimming teams for these two schools.

During the winter we all went to Hoyt Park for skating, sledding, and bobsledding down the huge iced hill that led onto a big natural pond basin that had been carefully flooded for use throughout the winter. Everyone gathered there on Saturdays and Sundays. My father taught me figure skating there and was keen to have me join the competition in racing on skates.

Financing of College Education

When it came to the expense of college, my father said that, if I worked full time every summer for pay and worked board job for meals during the nine months of school, he would do his best to pay the rest of the bills for Jack and me to get us through college.

Thus, my second blessing besides genes was to have good parents who instilled good work and play habits and church habits and assured us that they would help us financially on anything else that was necessary to achieve our objectives.

Retrospect

It fascinated me to learn that just before Rose Kennedy died at the age of 104 in January 1995, she had pictured her life as a series of "agonies and ecstasies." I had just written this chapter using those same headings.

The Ecstasies
(July 1, 1941–February 1, 1942)

Internship

Suddenly the ecstasy started with my internship at Cleveland City Hospital in Cleveland, Ohio. After nineteen years of formal studying and seven costly years of college education, I found myself starting my internship as a physician. At last, I had my own patients under the teaching and supervision of a fourth-year resident in internal medicine and a senior attendant who also had his own appointment with Case Western Reserve Medical School and his own private practice in Cleveland.

I shifted, for the first time in my life, from writing and memorizing lecture notes to study for examinations to studying at the hospital medical library for the simple purpose of learning to make the correct diagnosis and save the patient's life with the latest, best treatment. It was one of the greatest thrills of my life.

The fact that I was also eventually going to use this knowledge to take my medical specialty examinations, oral and written, for the American Board of Internal Medicine was four or five years away and was only a thought for the future.

We alternated with a partner being "on call" for nights and weekends. There were also first, second, and third call doctors in case we should have far more patients descend upon the hospital than one intern could handle. We were not paid a cent because the best internship paid nothing at that time. Hospitals with inferior teaching programs had to pay whatever they could to interns and residents so that hospitalized patients could be cared for by the attending physician in private practice. The interns were given board, room, and laundry *if they lived in the hospital*. Most of us were not yet married, and we spent what few minutes we could find playing tennis on the hospital tennis court and playing golf on the nearest and cheapest municipal golf course. We also had endless house staff social gatherings, so we were *never* lonely.

For example, one woman physician's room was at the entrance from the hospital catacombs (underground passageways) to the staff quarters. It seemed as though *everyone* stopped into her room to relax and socialize on their way back from seeing patients on the wards and in the outpatient building, whether she was there or not. We also had staff picnics at various parks. If a woman resident could be interested in going swimming (bribed with smiling, sweet talk, and alcohol) at one of these picnics, she could plan on being stripped of her bathing suit while she was in the water. (The women residents not infrequently stripped the males, also.) The stripped doctor was told that if he or she wanted to dress, they would find clothes and a towel up on the beach, etc.

We all knew that we could be drafted into the armed services and continually monitored each other's latest mail on the subject. The parties in our rooms in the interns' quarters in the evenings would suddenly and unexpectedly be interrupted by a firecracker going off in the party room. When the firecracker went off under your chair, it created a deep sense of uneasiness and the feeling that it was time to leave the room. A squadron of doctors would then peel off to march down the halls of the interns' quarters, throwing lighted firecrackers through the open transoms of sleeping doctors' rooms from the first floor up to the fifth floor. On the fifth floor, some of the most sedate doctors, now changed by alcohol and the ecstasy of socializing, would form off into "chariots." The chariots were actually big canvas laundry carts. More and more doctors would get into these carts while others would push the "chariots" in races down the hall. Occasionally, the person in the chariot was threatened with being abandoned by the pusher after he had headed the chariot toward the stairs at the end of the hall. The "finalists" would then assemble on the roof of the hospital for the final ceremony. The final ceremony was to shoot lighted

206

Roman candles and skyrockets off the top of the hospital and into the open (hopefully) windows of houses surrounding the hospital.

The startled resident of the house was awakened by a skyrocket coming through his bedroom window. If he was intelligent, he would get hold of the hospital superintendent the next morning to express to him his concern about all the possibilities of this wild action. Mr. Bugbee, the superintendent, would then call a staff meeting first thing in the morning, and his preamble would be a statement of his understanding that we were working twenty-four hours a day, seven days a week, for no pay and might soon go off to be killed in World War II. He would then urge us with various degrees of exhortation to understand that the surrounding neighbors could exert considerable pressure if they were at all organized to produce drastic changes for the worse for the doctors, our patients, and the hospital unless we curbed this late night outreach program. With great diligence, I finally found that the source of all these fireworks was a huge trunk under the bed of the chief resident of psychiatry.

The acquisition of this fact turned out to be of great help to me. A few days after I was married, I was in bed in our tiny nonbedroom apartment, still very much on honeymoon and on second call when, at 1:00 A.M., a nurse in psychiatry called and asked me to come to the hospital (five blocks away). She needed me to write an order for chloral hydrate to aid a patient in getting to sleep. When I refused as tactfully as possible without trying to explain why my wife needed me at home at that moment more than the nurse did, she threatened to call the chief resident in psychiatry and tell him that I had refused to come over. With my secret of who owned and dispensed the fireworks as a "hidden passion," I told her to feel free to call him. I told her that she could tell him, if necessary, that I was positive that he would not require me to come over that evening but could find an alternative way to get the patient the chloral hydrate (for example, a verbal order from him that he could sign the next morning). It came as no surprise to me that this wise psychiatric resident never reprimanded me.

The Agonies

World War II

The pace of our lives changed sharply when the Japanese shot up and bombed Pearl Harbor in Oahu at 7:55 A.M. on December 7, 1941. There were nineteen United States ships in this little harbor, including eight battleships! Suddenly, the Industrial Revolution accelerated in the United States and the employees in the hospital were drained off by highly paid jobs, most of which paid far more than any intern or resident physician received. Furthermore, these employees had started to earn a good living sometimes before they even finished high school and had been earning a good salary for the eight years that the doctors were earning nothing. Physicians were subjected to a quick draft and possible early death. Eighteen members of my graduation class from medical school were killed, and the number one man in our class scholastically was killed first.

Confined to Bed for One Year

Just as my wife Mary-Martha had found a job in Cleveland (moving from New Haven, Connecticut, to Cleveland) and we were in our second month of making a wonderful adjustment to our marriage, I was told that I had minimal tuberculosis of both lungs and would have to go to bed for an unknown period of time but probably at least one year in the Lowman Memorial Tuberculosis Pavilion of Cleveland City Hospital.

Since there were no drugs available at that time for treatment of civilians with tuberculosis, I was ordered to never sit up in bed (to speed the healing of my lungs) and put on a high-milk

208

intake to furnish calcium to "help calcify" my tuberculous lesions.

Since I had *minimal* tuberculosis and most patients in the hospital had advanced tuberculosis with sputum loaded with active tubercle bacilli, I was put in solitary confinement in a small room on the top floor of the TB sanitarium with a window that gave me a view of twenty-six bricks in an adjacent brick wall.

When criminals were put in solitary confinement at that time to inflict upon them the worst possible treatment for their sins, they were allowed to be up and around without use of bed-pans, urinals, and lying down to eat. One woman resident in internal medicine who was found to have tuberculosis refused admission to the hospital and had to see a psychiatrist for some time. I gradually found out that the non-doctor patients developed a high incidence of chronic alcoholism. Schizophrenia was a common problem. Indeed, one of the more exciting aspects of living in this environment was the sudden screaming of a patient in the room next in the middle of the night because he was standing at the window and was positive he saw fire trucks and screamed, "Fire, fire, fire!" We never knew for sure whether this really was a fire or whether another person had cracked up. Fortunately, it was never a fire. It was always a case of schizophrenia.

I will always remember my first few nights in the hospital. The first night my door and that of the room across the hall from me were open. The patient was dying and did die of his tuberculosis that evening but gave a chillingly extremely realistic description, as he died, of leaving his body and going to heaven where he met Saint Peter and Jesus Christ. The next day the patient who was in the room at the foot of my bed also died of tuberculosis. The next day the man in the room at the head of my bed died of tuberculosis.

The next day a handsome, six-foot-tall man dropped in to see me in his walk down the hall. He was a fellow patient. He asked me how long I had been in the hospital, and I said only a few days. I explained to him rather fervently, however, that I only had minimal tuberculosis in my two lungs and therefore I thought everything would go well. He told me that he had been

209

admitted with only minimal tuberculosis in one lung, had then spent two years in the hospital at strict bed rest and the next day was going to have a thoracoplasty (an operation to *permanently collapse most of the ribs on one side* of the chest to give that lung permanent rest).

Since the war industry had drained off many of the maintenance employees who delivered and washed dishes, etc., my meals came to me on a cart that had been used to get there from the other side of the hospital on that floor and so I had cold food three times a day for one year. I saw a nurse for a few minutes twice a day. Fortunately, my wife was allowed to see me after she had dinner each evening.

Spiritual Evolution

With the realization that I could not plan on living for any definite period of time or even get out of the hospital on any particular date, and an insurance man had told me that the death rate was extremely high from tuberculosis, I had plenty of motivation and plenty of time (24 hours a day, 365 days a year) to rethink my life and to develop the best possible religion to help me maintain my sanity and maximum happiness under these circumstances.

The Old Testament

Gradually, I realized that the Old Testament of the Bible presented what appeared to me to be an arbitrary and frequently vindictive God who freely and horribly punished "enemies" and assigned blame, much of which was irretrievable and unforgivable. Then, I gradually evolved a more realistic and happier religion of my own to explain the God of the Old Testament and the much nicer Christ of the New Testament.

The God of the Old Testament largely represented old and impartial physical laws that could be "obeyed" or not obeyed. If they were not obeyed, an understandable and possibly fatal punishment could be expected. For example, the law of gravity is understandable. Without the law of gravity, our lives would be chaotic and we could eventually be lost in space if we tried to take a walk. If we defy the law of gravity by jumping off a cliff, we could understandably be permanently disabled or killed. Nevertheless, we had to learn this law and its consequences to be free of unfavorable consequences. If we learned the law and "obeyed" it, we could have all sorts of beneficial circumstances, such as being able to drain the sink when through using it.

The New Testament

It began to occur to me that the New Testament with the introduction of Christ similarly introduced a large number of laws that we must learn and use properly if we are to enjoy an optimum life. Now I realized that God would not have to be convinced by pleading that we should win a football game rather than the opposing team or that our country should win in a war over another country. Similarly, if a man walked off a cliff and died, he was not killed because God "did it to him." With the new interpersonal laws presented mostly in the New Testament with Christ, I realized that God loved all of us and, because of this love, gave His only Son in the flesh as a human being to walk on this earth and live with us so that He would experience all our problems directly and thus be in the ideal position to help His fellowman. This expression of the highest possible life was obviously an action of the unconditional love of God and Christ.

Doing unto others what we want others to do to us requires work on our part and a curbing of natural tendencies to selfishness, greed, anger, etc. (original survival mechanisms). If we constantly give ourselves to helping others, we are directly and indirectly aiding progress in the civilization on this planet. Thus, to "love" others requires a conscious and deliberate giving to others to aid them to achieve the most civilized or "spiritual" evolution. Since this commitment to the welfare of others, because of our God-given love of man and his spiritual evolution, is not dependent upon the perfection of our eyesight, hearing, strength, etc., we can evolve spiritually until the day we die.

Since death is inevitable and will stop all these activities, how one uses his time daily assumes an increased importance day by day, hour by hour, and minute by minute.

It doesn't matter whether the person who provides these services is a minister, a physician, a nurse, a businessman, a street cleaner, a housemaid, or a dime store clerk. The question that each of these workers needs to ask himself or herself each day is how he or she can best serve others.

It is of interest that suddenly the largest, most successful corporations today are stressing that the reason they are becoming successful is because they are daily asking all their employees for answers to the question of how the company can best serve their customers. Thus, the best relationships in life are those that are mutually beneficial.

It is of interest that the Marquis *Who's Who in America* and *Who's Who in the World*, etc., state that "an individual biographical record in one of these volumes is limited to those individuals who have demonstrated outstanding achievement in their own fields of endeavor and who have therefore contributed significantly to the betterment of contemporary society."

The Church and Friends
Bob McNamara and Tom Lilly

When we went back to Ann Arbor for my internship and residency at the University Hospital, we became members of the First Presbyterian church in Ann Arbor. This membership afforded us many more developmental opportunities.

Shortly after we joined the First Presbyterian church in Ann Arbor, I accepted a request to become a member of the board of trustees and elders of that church. Since my entire income was about $1,200 a year, I am certain that I was not put on the board of trustees for financial reasons unless they wanted a complete spread of all the various incomes in the governing board. At my second meeting of the board, I was introduced to a young man who had just been appointed to take the place of one of the previous members who had moved to California. I asked him what he did in life. He said that he was a "controller." I asked him what a controller was, and he said it was sort of a glorified accountant. His name was Robert McNamara. In the thirteen years that I was on the board of trustees and elders with Bob, he rose eventually to become president of the Ford Motor Company.

One year I was in charge of the fundraising to raise money to add a Sunday school wing and, much to my embarrassment, found that my two sublieutenants were the president of Ford Motor Company and his best friend, Tom Lilly, who was president of Ford International at that time. Since they were good friends of mine, I told them that this was ridiculous and I thought one of them should be in charge and I would be a "gopher." They said no, that was exactly the way they wanted it. They wanted me to do the work and they would sit by and criticize.

During one of those years on the board of trustees, I found myself waiting at LaGuardia Airport after having arrived early for my return flight to Detroit Metro Airport. Who should walk up to sit with me but Bob McNamara? We sat together on the plane all the way home, and I learned how he had been recruited as one of the original "whiz kids" from the School of Business Administration at Harvard. One of the many reasons he left the faculty and came to the Ford Motor Company was that he and his wife were caught in a polio epidemic and were left with large bills to pay on a small academic salary. I was very impressed with Bob's intelligence and his remarkable ability to speak extemporaneously on almost any business subject as though he had thought it over very carefully and memorized it and put it on a computer.

Later, Bob McNamara was chosen by Pres. John F. Kennedy to be his secretary of defense. He was then hired by the World Bank to be head of the World Bank. Later he moved back to Washington, where he does some consulting practice. About ten years ago, I wrote him a letter. His reply came back in an envelope addressed to me in pencil with the answers to my questions pencilled onto the letter that I had typewritten to him. Many members of the board of trustees were entrepreneurs with their own businesses. It gave me an opportunity to learn a great deal from them.

213

Conclusion

I was encouraged by friends to write my memoirs because of my "stories," not to present seventy-eight years of details of my life.

It occurred to me, in reviewing memories of my life in anticipation of writing an autobiography, that some events were much more memorable than others. These events frequently were characterized by being related to unusual people in my life or to unusual messages (to change or guide my life) by less-well-known people.

I then realized that I have written the description of the evolution of a soul from birth to retirement at age seventy-eight from patient care, teaching as a professor of medicine, and medical research. Finally, it occurred to me that I have developed a huge extended family of former trainees who come from or live in almost every country in the world. Therefore, for better or for worse, I have encouraged a large number of outstanding people with a role model of the evolution of a soul.

It also occurred to me that much of the excitement of my life (and of this book) is related to the outstanding people with whom I have shared a friendship. All of these friends have taught me a great deal and have become "soul mates."

A major part of my soul, however, is a fifty-three-year marriage to my wife and beloved "soul mate" Mary-Martha, our three children, six grandchildren, and a steady acquisition of new friends in Ann Arbor and in Grosse Pointe (and the Grosse Pointe Memorial church) with constant changes in our lives.

I hope that the reader will see how exciting, funny, and rewarding life has been as this person evolved spiritually.

I was intrigued by the *Westminster "Interpreter's Bible"* and gradually bought all the volumes one at a time. I read these using my twenty-minute-a-day "quiet time" in the early mornings before praying. These interpretations of the Old Testament and the New Testament were written by the most outstanding theologians in the world at that time. I am sure that they helped me in my spiritual evolution, but I am not positive how. Also, I have known many people who are much further along in their spiritual development than I who have never heard of the *Interpreter's Bible*.

I also read the popular literature in psychiatry, such as *Love against Hate*. The most recent book that I have read twenty-three times is M. Scott Peck's *The Road Less Traveled*. This has been the most helpful book for me and my patients. The most recent *New York Times* bestsellers, *The Celestine Prophecy, Embraced by the Light*, and *The Care of the Soul* and *Soul Mates* by Thomas More have helped me to continue to evolve spiritually. I am still discouraged, however, at how slow my progress is and how little time I spend listening to the problems of others, now that I have retired (two months ago) from the position of practicing internal medicine and thyroidology for the second time.

Appendixes

Appendix 1

Letter from Peter Ward

The University of Michigan
Medical School

DEPARTMENT OF PATHOLOGY

Peter A. Ward. M.D.
Godfrey D. Stobbe Professor
 of Pathology
Professor and Chairman

22 January 1993

William H. Beierwaltes, M.D.
Professor Emeritus
917 Whittier
Grosse Pointe Park, Michigan 48230

Dear Bill:

I am sorry that I could not have been present at the ceremony on Friday, January 22nd, in which the University received from Cytogen the first clinically approved kit for ^{111}In-antibody imaging of colorectal tumors. I understand this ceremony appropriately acknowledged your pioneering efforts that made this technology a reality in the clinical setting. It is a rare instance when one can be publicly acknowledged as the one individual who has, in essence, been responsible for establishment of a new specialty in the field of medicine

Again, my congratulations to you

Best regards.

Sincerely,

Peter A. Ward, M.D.

PAW/mat
cc: Giles G. Bole, Jr., M.D.
        Thomas J, McKearn, M.D., Ph.D.
        Dr. Richard Wahl
        Tadataka Yamada, M.D.
50121924.ltr

Appendix 2

University of Michigan Distinguished Faculty Award, 1982

WILLIAM H. BEIERWALTES

Professor of Internal Medicine

The world has applauded your research. You have been acclaimed a Pioneer in Nuclear Medicine because of your many accomplishments that have helped to forge Nuclear Medicine into a scientific discipline. Your textbook, The Clinical Use of Radioisotopes, was the first of its kind, and it has set the tenor for the practical use of radioactivity, for transforming basic discoveries into helping sick people. From the application of radioiodine to diseases of the thyroid to the synthesis of new radiopharmaceuticals for diagnosis and treatment of disorders in the adrenal gland, your investigations have been models to guide others. Your devotion to basic science and your untiring efforts have made The University of Michigan one of the few centers for Positron Emission Tomography in the country.

Your blending of an atmosphere of enthusiasm and inquiry with a dynamic approach to research, has attracted many gifted scientists to study under your guidance. Your provocative style has inspired learning for many students. The consequential interaction of ideas and the aggregation of talent has earned universal respect for you.

As the chief, you have organized and developed a division in which the highest levels of scholarship and education are sought. At the same time, expert and diligent medical care is given to thousands of patients. You have much enhanced the prestige of your University.

To further honor your many accomplishments, the University takes great pleasure in bestowing upon you its Distinguished Faculty Award.

Appendix 3

Two examples of how a patient's life was saved as a result of my attendance at meetings of the Association of American Physicians:

1. Parkinson's disease patient

   One evening when I came home from the Association of American Physicians meeting in Atlantic City, Mary-Martha and I went to the Town Club in Ann Arbor for dinner. We saw our friends, Harold and Vi Goldman. It occurred to me that Harold's Parkinson's disease had been progressive. I, therefore, told him that I had witnessed Cotzias, professor of neurology at Brookhaven National Laboratories, present the markedly beneficial effect of the administration of levodopa by mouth. I asked Harold to tell his neurologist (Russ De Jong) and I would call Cotzias to get the pills. As a result, Harold was the first patient, in at least the state of Michigan, to be treated with levodopa. He improved 90% within weeks. Harold then confided in me that one week before I talked to him he had promised himself that, unless a new successful treatment was offered him, he would commit suicide in two weeks.

2. Toxoplasmosis of the brain

   Just I entered my office at University Hospital in Ann Arbor on the afternoon of the last day of the meetings, a general practitioner in the upper peninsula of Michigan called me about a patient of his with proven toxoplasmosis of the brain. He said, "Bill, you will think I am silly to call but I have wonderful and attractive young woman patient we have proved to have encephalitis caused by the protozoan infection, toxoplasmosis. I know there is no successful treatment of this condition but I cannot let her die without at least making a phone call to see if you have heard of any new treatment." He was surprised to hear me state, "It just happens that I witnessed a presentation of the first successful treatment of toxoplasmosis with active chorioretinitis this morning." The treatment was pyrimethamine and sulfadiazine for a month. A good clinical response occurs in about two-thirds of such patients. Prednisone may blunt the inflammatory response of the retina.

   Again, we believe that this patient was at least the first patient in the state of Michigan to be so treated and successfully.